THE OBU MANIFESTOS

THE
OBU
MANIFESTOS

BY
OBU

MANIFESTOS 1–42
NOVEMBER 2016 – MARCH 2017

Dispatches Editions

Some of these Manifestos have appeared previously at *Dispatches from the Poetry Wars,*
http://dispatchespoetry.com/home/recent/news

Dispatches Editions
11 Conrad Ave.
Toronto Ontario M6G 3G4
Canada

Dispatches Editions is an imprint of Spuyten Duyvil Press
http://www.spuytenduyvil.net/

ISBN 978-1-944682-75-0

LIBRARY OF CONGRESS CATALOGING-IN-PUBLICATION DATA APPLIED FOR

OBU Manifestos

1-42

OBU Manifesto #1

OBU IS A NATIONAL ORGANIZATION SUPPORTING SOCIAL JUSTICE AND DEMOCRACY and opposing tyranny, oligarchy, and racism. It is extraordinary in its effectiveness, cohesiveness, commitment, and imagination.

OBU does not exist.

OBU will defend immigrants from deportation. OBU members will put their bodies and souls on the line to defend their immigrant brothers and sisters.

OBU will defend all stigmatized peoples from hate crimes. They will not permit these crimes to happen in their communities or anywhere in this country. OBU will defend black people from police violence. OBU will protect Muslims, Jews, LBGQT people, women, Native peoples, and the disabled from reactionary violence.

OBU will come with bodies, minds, and lawyers to prevent this violence; and, if it happens, to provide justice.

OBU is One Big Union

OBU *is* black, Muslim, Jewish, LBGQT, female (and male, and trans), white, Asian, Christian, Native, and disabled. OBU believes in the dignity and rights of all human beings.

OBU is a figment of our imagination.

OBU is everywhere.

OBU will bring the battle relentlessly against the oligarchy and plutocracy that characterize the American economic-political system.

OBU is working people across the United States.

OBU fights for the Earth, for health-providing ecosystems, and for sustainable economies that allow the planet and its inhabitants to thrive.

OBU is Oligarchy Busters United

OBU is workers in unions and workers not in unions and people without jobs.

OBU believes in the value and dignity of all human labor. OBU believes that all work should be fairly remunerated.

OBU does not believe that the fiction called *The Market* should determine what forms of work have value and which do not.

OBU will spread across the country like a mighty stream and remove the unjust from positions of power.

OBU values righteous anger at oppression and greed. OBU does not value contempt or hatred.

OBU opposes hypocrisy in all guises and locations.

OBU is the idea whose time must come.

OBU Manifesto #2

OBU LISTENS TO EVERYONE WHO OPPOSES OLIGARCHY—EVEN TRUMP SUPPORTERS. These are opponents who will be allies.

OBU will sponsor exchange programs. OBUs will stay in red zones for month or two stints, talking and listening, sharing species membership, configuring new American identities. And OBU will host curious red zone denizens to come to our urban bubbles to do the same.

OBU does not believe that all differences can be reconciled, but we will do the best we can. We talk and we listen.

OBU believes that the economic analysis of many Trump voters is correct. The white working class—together with the entire American working class—has been exploited, abandoned, and forgotten. The U.S. is an oligarchy ruled by and for the benefit of the wealthy and their adjuncts in the bourgeois professional classes. Certain sectors of Trump voters know this as well or better than we do. OBU hopes that ongoing conversation will help sever this economic and class analysis from the stigmatizations of racial-ethnic-religious-gender minorities that accompany it in the Trump ideological-strategic garbage dump.

OBU does not in any way accept this racism, etc. It does not believe that civil or loving conversation can cure deeply held racist-xenophobic-homophobic, etc. attitudes.

OBU is one of the granddaughters of the Beloved Community of the Civil Rights Movement.

OBU is One Big Union

OBU is in the air searching for places to land.

OBU creates unities across class and race and gender and employment status. If you recognize the injustice of the economic system, you are OBU. If you are determined to act, you are OBU.

OBU insists on individual responsibility. We are all responsible to act with compassion. We are all responsible to work to create solidarities.

OBU reserves its most disgusted derision for those who believe their main responsibility is to increase their personal wealth.

OBU is descended from the International Workers of the World, the original "One Big Union."

OBU believes the answer is not in heaven, that we should say, who can go up to heaven to bring it down for us? OBU believes the answer is very close to us.

Where two or more are gathered, there is OBU.

OBU is Oligarchy Busters United

OBU says, catch up on your sleep whenever you can.

OBU is anger and love and energy and unwavering commitment.

OBU Manifesto #3

OBU IS WHAT IT WILL BE.

OBU is everywhere but OBU is not the only game in town. OBU supports and works with all groups that fight oligarchy and that defend those who are attacked.

All groups that fight oligarchy and defend those who are attacked and work for the power of working people are OBU.

OBU is the negation and the affirmation.

OBU is the articulation and the action.

OBU is webs of solidarity. OBU is the love that flourishes in moments of darkness.

OBU understands despair and does not succumb.

OBU IS ONE BIG UNION

OBU believes that every meeting must end with everyone knowing what they are to do before the next meeting.

OBU also embraces those who don't know what to do before the next meeting.

OBU cannot believe that in its lifetime it ever would have witnessed such a thing as the 2016 election.

OBU refuses to accept the subversion of democracy.

OBU could not believe that ever in its lifetime it would witness such a thing as the 2000 election.

But it did. And it did.

Many things have happened in the lifetimes of OBU that can't be believed.

But here we are.

William Blake wrote that "one law for the lion and the lamb is oppression," but OBU does not see how this is relevant. We are all people–we are not divided into subspecies of predators and prey.

OBU knows that capital divides people into predators and prey.

OBU is still capable of surprise. What will be the next surprise?

OBU IS OLIGARCHY BUSTERS UNITED

OBU is every pragmatic alliance that can be made to dismantle or delay the onslaught of awful legislation the new government will unleash on us to destroy the rights of workers, women, and minorities.

OBU is the bonds of support that will keep people from hunger and homelessness.

OBU is money, generosity, the creation of institutions, the building of power.

OBU is friendship and respect across all faction.

OBU Manifesto #4

OBU ASKS–AFTER WILLIAM BLAKE–WHY SHOULD THE "CUT WORM FORGIVE THE PLOW"?

OBU answers, Because it's a worm! It fertilizes soil. And anyway, both halves of it live.

But OBU speaks as people, not as worms. Two parts of a severed man or woman cannot live again.

OBU notes that two parts of a severed country, a country severed by the plow of global capital and lacerated by histories of stigmatizing, humiliating, oppressing, and assaulting weaker social groups cannot easily or quickly be healed.

OBU believes that forgiveness must be earned.

But OBU also believes that deeper bonds of human connection and recognition can be located, although they seem well-hidden.

OBU is not sure it knows what is meant by *recognition*. It seems the wrong word for what it designates. To "know again"? As if one knew before? What is that prior knowledge?

To know the "other," OBU is certain, means to know his/her history. And then, one can say, ok, I've seen that before... not *that* history exactly, but something akin to that. That story is familiar. One ought to hesitate before saying, yes, that story is just like my story or just like some other story I've heard. The other will say, "Bullshit. Fine. Your people have suffered; my people have suffered. But my history is what is at issue *now*, because the consequences of that historical oppression still constitute the basic facts of my experience. Your history, on the other hand, has ceased to wound you. Or ceased, at least, in ways you can immediately recognize."

OBU is One Big Union?

And so, OBU reasons, to *recognize* the other is one step. The further step is–what word can we use?–to *"cognize"* the other. Not to know again, but to know anew, to know, perhaps not as unique, but certainly as particular–that there is a particular and not universal history that has brought the other to where they are.

And yet, OBU recognizes, the histories are kin. The capacities to suffer and to inflict suffering have their places in all histories. They are generalizable. Others' histories must be recognized.

OBU remembers that *because* we were slaves in Egypt, we are obligated to be just to the stranger. And all of us were slaves. All of us were in "the narrow place." That is the point of the story.

And what if one's own group has played the role of Blake's plow in recent history, and cut through the bodies of others? Shall we ask for forgiveness? Or shall we, as another of Blake's proverbs advises, "drive our cart and plow over the bones of the dead"? Why dwell on the past? Forget and move forward. And is either of these remedies sufficient?

OBU remembers also Walter Benjamin's admonition that if the oppressor triumphs, "even the dead will not be safe."

OBU is Oligarachy Busters United?

OBU wonders what songs we know? What songs can we sing together? Do the old labor and folk and civil rights songs still work? When we're in the street, confronting power, what will we sing? Can we make new songs? Can we make new poems?

OBU is frustrated by the insipid, mindless chants that fill the air during demonstrations. If we're going to win this, we need good songs.

And we could use some good poems.

What about, "When will we be paid– for the work we've done?"

OBU says, Google it if you don't know it.

OBU Manifesto #5

OBU PERFORMS MOMENTOUS ACTS OF POLITICAL THEATER.

OBU causes buildings to levitate for freedom.

OBU is the Orchestra Bringing Unraveling to all injustice.

OBU is the music in your head that persuades you that happiness is possible.

Every person alive and dead is at the center of OBU's story.

OBU is a pompous sack of manure. Spread it and let it nourish the soil of the cities and towns. Sunlight and rain will oxidize the pomposity. New trees will grow. The only problem will lie in grasping the complexities of their roots and branches.

OBU is Oafish Bunglers Undulating. OBU is unequal to the tasks that face us.

OBU is our only hope.

OBU is willing to violate all the laws of nature to achieve justice.

OBU's Mad Genius Monkeys and Dolphins are working on how to do this.

OBU IS ONE BIG UNION

OBU is divided on this.

Oligarchy and oppression can be fought without supplementary readings. But OBU believes that we need our ghosts. The more wise ghosts we have, the surer we'll be in our struggle.

OBU postpones and delays and defers. Now is not the right time, it avers. Now is the time for understanding time. Time is lending itself. When must we pay it back? OBU says that many things are now imperative. OBU calls for immediate action. OBU posts its ruminative demands on FaceBook. OBU is part of a community of shock. OBU says, we are not surprised this happened, it was always implicit in a racist system. OBU says the inconceivable has happened; a conman buffoon has found the racist integuments of the American political corpus and ripped them off like new intestines spewing excrement to the vast entertainment of millions.

OBU contends that if you don't know what a word means, look it up.

OBU is divided on this.

OBU believes that the defunding of public education from K through college is having exactly the effect that was intended: the contempt for knowledge, the lack of understanding of how knowledge is acquired, the deep suspicion of sustained thinking, the fear of other ways of thinking and living, the vulnerability to political whims (from Obama's vacuous "Hope" directly to the Tea Party and to Trump's poisonous charisma), apathy, addiction to opioids.

OBU read that the lower the average educational level, the more likely was a county to vote for Trump.

OBU does not believe that "postmodern" thinking, art, poetry, and philosophy or the various forms of "identity" politics and scholarship–African American studies, gender studies, various ethnicity studies, etc.–are what have brought universities (and the Left) to cultural irrelevance, or somewhere on the road to it. It may be that these have not been especially effective as politics over the past twenty or thirty years. But then, who or what has? Democratic Party technocratic, austerity Liberalism has deepened the power of oligarchy–an oligarchy without overt racism, in contrast to the Republican Party version.

OBU IS (STILL) OLIGARCHY BUSTERS UNITED

OBU knows magic tricks. OBU knows the date and time of every lunar and solar eclipse. OBU has memorized the tides and can identify clouds, trees, and musical chords. OBU impersonates new elements on the Periodic Table.

But will OBU learn to use firearms?

OBU can recite extended passages from the Old and New Testaments, from the Koran, and from the canonical books of Hindu, Jain, Bahai, Parsee, Buddhist, Shinto, Confucian, Mayan, Iroquois, Ashanti, and Mormon traditions. OBU feels at home in all places of worship.

OBU has a newly engineered translation chip planted behind the left eye that allows OBU to understand and speak all human languages.

OBU believes in non-violence. But it likewise believes those who are attacked in their exercise of non-violence have the inalienable right to self-defense. OBU will seek to practice non-violence even when attacked and it will earnestly encourage others to do so. But it will not condemn those who honorably defend themselves and their loved ones and communities in legitimate acts of protection.

Now can we move forward?

OBU Manifesto #6

OBU KNOWS THAT SOMEONE IN THE PAST ALREADY UNDERSTOOD THE CRISES WE'RE facing today.

The injustices of the past continue and repeat themselves, with variations. The mistakes, stupidities, and brutalities repeat themselves. The paths not taken and the roads taken into chaos and horror all have been traveled or not traveled.

And yet the present remains unprecedented and mysterious, and the question facing us always is what are we going to *do*?

OBU believes that great learning is necessary. But it's debatable how much.

OBU believes that intellectuals, scholars, artists and all their ideas and products are good and beneficial to the struggle. And that means ALL, no matter how apparently esoteric, hermetic, historical, avant, post-avant, incomprehensible, and without clear social value.

OBU contends that the production of beauty and knowledge is the production of joy, and the production of difficulty is also the production of joy–immediate for some, not-yet-arrived for others.

Working to understand something has political value.

OBU also believes that intellectuals, scholars, poets, and artists should at times get off their butts, disengage from their projects, and really kick in to the struggle–simply as citizens and human beings, with no special privilege.

OBU IS ONE BIG UNION

OBU believes that intellectuals should not suppose that the radical politics of their writing is sufficient.

OBU contends that if you love doing theory, art, poetry, the production of knowledge of all sorts, then that's what you should do. It has inherent value. It is a utopian model of non-alienated labor (even as it is performed in the context of a larger system of alienated and exploited labor).

But, OBU contends that if you want to do politics, then there is no alternative but– to do politics.

And "doing politics" means creating bases of actual power that can oppose the dominant powers: capital, its institutions and supporters.

OBU is Oligarchy Busters United

OBU recognizes the irony of these calls to action enclosed in the form of a Manifesto.

OBU recognizes the obvious questions that must be posed to it: Who is speaking? To whom is "who" speaking? How will these messages be disseminated? How will they be acted on?

OBU must ask, is the Manifesto itself just an artistic form, an artistic pleasure?

OBU can tell you sincerely, it is a pleasure–... but is it more?

Ludwig Wittgenstein wrote that his writing was like a ladder which, after you climbed it, you should throw away.

OBU cannot answer the question exactly of how the Manifesto will ultimately contribute to a politics effectively fighting oligarchy. OBU can only reply that that will be up to its readers– but knows that this answer is a cop-out.

OBU is not sure it even likes people very much. There's a lot not to like. And OBU assumes that the feeling is mutual. But OBU knows that this is not the point.

OBU recalls that Hamlet said that if you treat everyone as they deserve, "Who should scape whipping?" Therefore, treat everyone better than they deserve.

And Alyosha said at the end of *The Brothers Karamazov*, "Be honest. But first, be kind."

OBU Manifesto #7

OBU IS ALSO THE KNOWLEDGE THAT THIS INCREDULOUS PAIN WILL MITIGATE; IT'S already doing so.

One tries to sustain it through serial outrage at every cabinet appointment. Oh my god look who's he's putting in charge of... whatever it is. But what did we expect? This is what it is. Use your imagination. This has happened. Let him select every venal, self-righteous, mean-spirited, unscrupulous American willing to serve and direct him.

OBU is not going anywhere.

At the first meeting of "What Now?" there were 200 people. At the second meeting there were 50. Whoever comes to the third meeting is OBU, the people ready to make real plans and carry them through for as long as it takes.

But the other people, who came to one meeting because of how they felt, that they must, at that moment, do something, make some gesture, be out of the house away from the TV and computer, must be with other people who feel the same– these people are OBU too. They'll be back. Once you take one action, however small, you'll take others more consequential.

OBU knows that these are times of consequence.

OBU strongly suspects that these times will call for quantities of courage, that each person will have to search for and summon this courage. Some will feel they were born for this, that their lives have always pointed toward these moments when boundless deep courage must be met and made into a vehicle and a structure. Others will be terrified that they won't be able to summon the courage, or able to keep it close and act on it if they find it. The acts of opposition and disobedience that may be called for will not be just political theater, not just symbolic. Oh, we'll take an arrest, we'll sit down on the street and polite police officers will guide us to tables where they'll book us and release us. People may be jailed for real, injured for real. OBU, for the most part, is not thrilled about this possibility, though some other parts of OBU are ready right now for this aspect of struggle.

OBU is committed to non-violence. OBU will not physically attack anyone.

But OBU is committed to the principle of the public, the public space, the commons. OBU will not permit what is public to be sold off and made into commodities. OBU will assemble. OBU will establish sites of education, culture, health care, leisure as public sites. Water is a public good; power is a public good; internet is a public good; transportation is a public good.

OBU does not contend that all property is theft. But OBU does contend that all privatization of public goods is theft.

OBU is ... ...

OBU's task is to imagine forms of solidarity that, in the present, have no power to exist.

OBU has reason to believe that the "news cycle" is an illusion whose purpose is to disempower.

One must know... What must one know? The claims and counter-claims, the attacks and defenses and counter-attacks. Representative R. wove his way to the fifteen yard line where he was shoved out of bounds by Chairwoman C with a minute-twenty left on the clock. Coach Q testified for seventeen hours regarding the scandal of the breakdown in his secondary. And the Mayors of Urbo and Blurbo exchanged comic insults regarding each other's masculinity/feminity, level of infection by tic-borne viruses, and sheer hunger for the devastating emptiness of American political life.

Almost all of what passes for "news," OBU asserts, is unnecessary and detrimental to understanding national or international political, economic, social, cultural, anthropological or scientific realities.

OBU does not exist.

Let's jump forward and look back. In which direction will we see OBU?

And yet, in this world, there are blessings still abundant. This chaos may be for blessing, since no one can control it. This cracked and porous world remains open.

But we have to be smart. We have to be open. We have to have courage and must overcome our fatigue. The only light we can throw ahead of us is our vision. Vision precedes light.

OBU is ...   ...

OBU Interlude #1

THE END IS SLOW. THE END IS ONRUSHING.

Everyone's lives go on just the same, pretty much,

except with new rules that say, mind your business and don't mess with it, and you'll be alright.

But it's out of your hands now.

If you fall through the floor now, it's a long drop.

An hour is still an hour, a day still a day, a year is a year.

But other measures fly through our bodies.

As we age in biological time, so slowly it seems (then slowly and too fast), the hurricanes of social time burst our levies and smash our houses.

And as we live our lives in a historical time whose truly significant changes we don't know how to register, our bodies decay and we are gone.

What's happening most quickly is happening slowly.

The change in the climate– it moves as slow as can be, a little bit this way a little bit more that way, and soon it will be here.

It's happening slowly and it's here now.

It's now.

But it can't be part of the news; the news is only what happens fast.

Unless there's a disaster.

And there's always a disaster, there's always been disaster.

The more disaster, the more news. But what moves slowly is never news.

Or which of the signs or symptoms will tell us that democracy is finally, truly gone?

OBU MANIFESTO #8

OBU MAKES ALLIANCES. OBU IS ALLIANCES.

OBU is contemplating, just for instance: there is a labor-oriented community social justice group affiliated with particular unions. It has proven able to mount mass demonstrations and civil disobedience actions. It is genuinely multi-racial and cross-class. It has enthusiastic young organizers with good training. Its long-term goals for building working-class power are broad and fundamental; but its actions all are focused on the immediate priorities of the unions. This group's organizing methods are lively and democratic; but its tactical, strategic, and wider communication practices are determined by a small steering committee and are tightly hierarchical.

OBU contemplates, on the other hand, a group with far looser organization. It is far more democratic. It meets, it holds forums, everyone present can speak and contribute to policy and strategy. Its meetings are long, but everyone tells what they feel and think. Its "breakout sessions"(intended to lead to action) accomplish very little. Its goals, ultimately, are vague in terms of accomplishing anything. But it allows everyone to participate... until the members lose interest because the group doesn't accomplish anything.

OBU asks, What did you expect?

OBU recognizes that in order to organize, a movement needs committees dedicated to organizing, and that an organizing committee is not a discussion group. Fair enough. There are plenty of forums for discussion. The organizing committee is there to go out into communities and organize–to reach people, talk with people and listen to them, persuade them that the situation is not hopeless, that their contributions are vital and will lead, eventually, to success. With other people, the goal is to move people out of complacency.

The weakness often of the group committed to organizing is a loss of vision. In order to keep momentum and morale, there must always be an event upcoming–a rally, a hearing, etc. The organizing committee is obsessed with its numbers. Who is coming? Are they confirmed? Who are they bringing? Do they need rides? What are the numbers? Can we put a thousand people in the street? How about twelve hundred?

OBU is One Big Union

But what, OBU asks, does it mean to be part of a Movement? What forms of shared understanding, knowledge, feeling (of anger, love, determination), personal relationship are necessary? And how are these to be achieved? And if the community organizing is linked to the work of a union, the purpose of that link must be absolutely clear. Why, it must be made clear again and again, is the power of organized labor utterly essential to an effective movement for social-economic-racial-gender justice?

And the union, OBU insists, must prove this fact always. In every one of its acts, even as it negotiates its own contracts, it must think in terms of communities outside its membership. It must be part of the One Big Union that does not yet exist.

And who has the energy to make this happen? How many pointless meetings must be endured before the Movement truly if uncertainly comes into being?

And who makes the plans, sets the priorities? And how is this determined? Who decides who will decide? The people who are most active decide. And they are people who either are on salary from some group (e.g. a union or non-profit) or otherwise have the time to put into the project. They are generally not people with other time-consuming jobs or extensive family responsibilities. In this model, the more you organize, the more you are listened to; the less you organize, the less your voice is attended. It's very much a corporate model. By doing the particular work that is most valued–organizing—you get closer and closer to being, finally, in the room where decisions are actually made.

But, OBU suggests, different tasks require different skills, and there are many tasks. The intense, but somewhat blindered labor of organizing can result in a forgetting of the larger aims.

OBU is Oligarchy Busters United

The connections, OBU insists, must always, *always* be made. We are doing this rally not because we're trying to make our numbers. It's not a game or an exercise. We're trying first, to put pressure on political-economic institutions so that they will change their policies and actions; and, second, we are trying to change the ideological climate so that the aims and efforts of the Movement will be more widely known and shared, so that future actions will be more powerful, so that a political force able to challenge oligarchy will be brought into being.

Because it sure as hell does not exist now. The existing union movement is not it. The existing anti-racism, anti-sexism, immigrant rights, LGBTQ rights movements are not it.

It is not necessary to have everything figured out. It is impossible to do so. But it is crucial to be trying to figure out how actions and ideologies connect. The overriding problem is oligarchy: poverty and inequality, the manipulations of racial bias, environmental destruction all are consequences of the dominion of a wealthy few.

It is astonishing, OBU considers, that the Left is as weak as it is, considering that its ideas and goals are, in fact, held so widely. But these are private views. We all believe we must fight poverty and inequality, racism, and environmental destruction. We are willing to sign petitions, post on FaceBook, give a little money, even occasionally give some time. But this is in the role of private citizen, compassionate and irate individual. In the aggregate, our primary public activities are work and consumption. We earn money and we spend money–as much as we are able. Our primary public role is participation in the market. And yet, the power of markets–that is, the presumed, fictive, usurped, and still quite real power–is at the center of our problems. That is our paradox. We are conjoined to the agent of our exploitation.

And so we must reimagine not just our political-economic world. We must reimagine ourselves.

OBU Manifesto #9

OBU IS IN MOURNING. THE WORLD REASSEMBLES ITSELF. THERE IS INCOMPREHENSION; there is relentless theorizing; there is the outraged energy that propels one to meeting after meeting as to "what shall we do?"... and people tell how they feel and how sad and angry and betrayed they are... and the plan we take out is: to feel sad and outraged and still have no plan.

And, gradually, OBU comes to the sense that there is still a world and that one is alive in it; that the world contains (for the moment) oxygen and water and sustenance; that its wars are (still, for the moment) elsewhere. The natural and human storms that seem now so proximate and inevitable have not yet burst on us–not here, not yet. The poor feel them, the Black feel them, the Native people feel them, immigrants feel them, the "middle class" feel them, the sexually abused and the gender abused of all groups feel them.

If OBU is not all of these, then it's nothing.

OBU feels these storms. If some of OBU have not yet reckoned with them personally, the whole of OBU knows they are close and they are here; they are soon and they are now. The distinctions have lost their importance.

OBU asks, does everyone feel only their own feelings? Is that really what it comes down to? Or are only certain people capable of feeling *with* others? Are some people able to step with imagination into another life? Are any people? Are most people?

It is the goal of our moral and intellectual education, OBU asserts, to prepare us to make that step of imagination into the lives of others.

And it is the further goal to teach us the humility of knowing that the imagination of another's life is not its actual experience. This is an ethics, a knowledge, an aesthetics, and a politics. One feels the suffering and oppression of the other; it is not, of course, the same feeling that the other–in her/his actual life–feels. But it is what allows and compels us to commit ourselves to stopping the suffering and injustice. And the "other," what is that? The *other* is another *person.*

OBU is One Big Union

How does one know, OBU asks, this other person–the person from another place, another neighborhood, another region, another social stratum, another historical experience? One can read. There are many wonderful novels, essays, poems, histories, pieces of journalism, films and documentaries that show people's lives. One should encounter all these texts and learn from them. For many people, this is the beginning.

But it can't be the conclusion. There must be places, institutions, organizations of real social contact. Social movements must be integrated–"integrated," that old term... before we knew about "diversity." When a place is merely "diverse," people of the various groups need not talk to each other, and the place will still be "diverse." *Integration* implies genuine relationships–the creation of a new social integrity out of the various constituent parts. Integration is the goal. Integration is the teacher.

"The sacred places where the races meet," says Leonard Cohen.

And out of integration–relation, knowledge, imagination, empathy, ethical and personal commitment—OBU hopes, will come solidarity.

Solidarity is the commitment to stay together in spite of setbacks. Solidarity is the willingness to take risks for each other. OBU will not say, at this point, what kind of risks may be faced. OBU does not know. OBU hopes they will not be too severe, but they may be severe. OBU knows that some people can summon more courage than can others, but OBU does not know how much courage will be needed, or what kind.

OBU is Oligarchy Busters United

The collective that is writing this document feels at times great lacks of both solidarity and courage. Perhaps that's why they're able to imagine them as vividly as they do.

OBU calls for a Mourn-In in every city and town. Come weeping, with large umbrellas and distribute tissue.... Come with bright large masks of Incredulity that a person of such social ignorance will oversee housing policy. Come weeping with circus prayer shawls... Come with Tinker toys and Legos and Lincoln Logs for the new Housing Secretary.... Come with Trump Fright Masks (are there any other kind?) so that Dr. C. can signify his fealty to his new Boss. Come weeping. And leave laughing, because this band of malicious, incompetent boobs will not succeed and will not stay in power.... if we unite and persevere

OBU Manifesto #10

OBU CALLS FOR NATIONAL DAYS OF MOURNING AND CONTRITION.

Whatever we've been doing, it ain't been fucking working. That includes the Obama years.

This great economic "recovery," says OBU, where is it really? These jobs that have increased so massively, what are they? Is it not clear, asks OBU, that the entire notion of work, of employment, has been transformed? There is no longer work, there are " gigs." You have a gig for a while, until a new technology or shift in location or new marketing strategy makes it unnecessary–for the employer. Capital no longer requires labor.

Capital no longer requires consumers. International and upscale markets will do all the consumption that's needed. Henry Ford's ancient insight is obsolete that the worker must be paid enough to afford to buy the product he produces.

Capital requires only more capital. Capital creates itself now. But you have to have capital to get capital.

The economy now is one of rent. We pay rent now to banks for the privilege of existing.

OBU submits that, in fact, we are more deeply fucked than we know, and Donald Trump has only just got on board. Begin the sentence with Donald Trump, but it's a long and difficult sentence and no one knows where it ends. We are living in an age of uncertain grammar.

And Trump really only picks things up in the middle.

OBU is forced to admit there are really only middles.

OBU calls for national days of mourning and contrition.

The victory at Standing Rock is glorious, whatever crushing defeat stands to follow.

The confession and plea for forgiveness on the part of the military veteran allies of the First Peoples at Standing Rock was one of the most profound and signifying moments in all American history. Even OBU could not imagine such a thing, and then it happened, as if some great wall had fallen.

And yet the wall still stands.

It is as if, OBU thinks, it doesn't matter what you do, it doesn't matter what you do, it doesn't matter what you do...

OBU is One Big Union

OBU is Oligarchy Busters United

OBU Manifesto #11

OBU BELIEVES THAT THE TECHNICAL PROBLEMS OF CAPITALISM CANNOT BE SOLVED by technical means. The problems are not technical.

When we speak of labor," "production," "consumption," markets" today, we refer to different things than were spoken of fifty years ago.

How does "work" work?

Neither technocrats nor demagogues will bring back work in the way it was.

OBU says the technocrats will not save us.

OBU says the people will not save us.

And no, not to worry, OBU is confident the intellectuals will not save us.

The artists and poets will not save us.

No avant-garde will save us.

But OBU says, let's think of "redeem" in its economic sense–to buy back, as if someone had put a lien on all of us. And that is, actually, exactly right. How much do people actually own? What is there that cannot be repossessed?

Everything we pay is rent and interest.

Our bodies are rented and temporary. Look at the secret amortization table of the cells. Every year we pay more, not less, in interest for the use of them, until the interest overwhelms the principle and we own nothing.

What kind of capital will redeem us?

Nothing will redeem us from our biological debt, of course–except, perhaps, children, memory, the effusions of soul in love, in art, in whatever passionate struggles whose material traces survive us.

But, OBU asks, is happiness possible in this world, while we live? And how do we think of happiness? Oh, if one *can* feel happiness, one should. Happiness is, in this world, an obligation. But what is the nature of happiness in a world predicated on predation? How exactly are the boundaries constructed within which happiness flourishes best? What forms of comfort and how obtained?

OBU recalls Frank O'Hara's line: "Happiness–the best and least of human attainments." To be happy is an obligation; but to increase the sum of happiness beyond one's private sphere is also an obligation.

Not to be happy all the time! What an absurd idea. But to have happiness not be precluded, to have happiness always as potential, which means as a power one might possess.

Happiness is power, says OBU, if properly understood. Happiness not experienced is potential, which may be a greater power.

Happiness may certainly be experienced under conditions of misery and oppression. Who is there so miserable that he or she cannot experience some happiness? There are times with loved ones; or moments when something is so funny that the world falls into an incongruous alignment of making sense in its madness; or times when you're just a little high and things feel pretty much as they should be, just a little better; or feeling crazy loving someone and knowing that person wants you too; or seeing one's children grow and seem to be happy and doing well, and you know how hard it is and yet it seems to be working out and that gives you such joy.

All these and other wonderful things happen in almost every life. But then, there are the losses: parents, brothers and sisters, friends, children who just can't make it, who sink underneath it, who are pushed under and can't climb back, and maybe they're gone or they're in a place you can't reach, and you know they're suffering, suffocating, diminished, pretending, grasping for weapons, meting out what they think is justice to anyone they can touch, and then beaten down by someone more powerful, or by the state or by chemicals or by promises.

Happiness will redeem us, thinks OBU, if only we can create for everyone the spaces around and between happiness, the boundaries of safety and strength within which and through which happiness flourishes.

OBU Manifesto #12

OBU IS THE MOVEMENT THAT DOES NOT EXIST.

If a group exists, it cannot be OBU.

No, that can't be right, exactly.

OBU is One Big UNION. Therefore it is an amalgam. It is the sticking together of things. The question OBU faces is, what makes it stick?

It is not for lack of feeling that OBU does not exist; it is for lack of proper *adhesion*.

It is so difficult, OBU laments, to keep everything in order

OBU is nourished by the fantasy that if only every factor could be accounted for, every counter-argument parried and turned to advantage, and no possible retort of "Well, what about...?" able to be wielded, then the Movement would fall into place, would click into place with a well-oiled and satisfying *Quod erat demonstrandum* and the (entirely non-violent) revolution could begin.

OBU IS ONE BIG UNION

But OBU has learned through painful experience that the better argument does not prevail. Or it *can* prevail, but not simply on its merits–there must be other forces.

OBU sees that one group is pretty good at on-the-ground organizing. But the group is run as a hierarchy, almost a corporate model, with committees that report to committees, a central planning unit, an obsession with tactics and a purposeful vagueness reg. strategy and broader vision. It fights for democracy but avoids democratic practice.

Other groups rely on feeling. OBU is told that we wept and prayed for Paris, but no one weeps and prays for Aleppo; and OBU thinks, how are weeping and praying an effective politics? If weeping and praying are the best we can offer, that tells us we're moving in a fruitless direction.

OBU IS OLIGARCHY BUSTERS UNITED

Oh, then you don't feel enough?! No! OBU feels plenty. There is providence in the fall of a sparrow, but one can't do anything about it– nor about Aleppo, at this moment. It doesn't matter how much you feel; it matters how you use emotion and reason and knowledge to create effective solidarities to battle oligarchy.

That's what it comes down to, OBU asserts. If you're not there, then where are you? Weeping for the lost souls of the day, and each day come new ones. And with every election, the oligarchy remains constant.

If the new henchman is Secretary of State or merely CEO of Exxon Mobil… what real difference? If he's not one, then he's the other, and another henchman will fill the vacancy.

OBU shares Stevie's fantasy in Joseph Conrad's *The Secret Agent*: to bring victim and oppressor (who is also himself a victim) together in a "bed of compassion"– if only we could talk with each other, interpret to and for each other, touch each other with heart, mind, and flesh, establish almost a communion or at least a new community or new sense of commonality… a touch… and then justice would begin. We would do this one by one, for that is the only way it can be done. And yet, of course, as Conrad points out, this method has "only the one disadvantage of being difficult of application on a large scale."

OK, OK, says OBU; well, then, we'll do it online. "Like" by "Like," "Share" by "Share." Solidarity and justice will go Viral! The world will be infected by them and thus redeemed. There is no resisting the Meme.

But the virus passes quicky, OBU notes, and the oligarchic organism emerges in good health. The great digital revolutions could not succeed. Occupy; the Arab Spring.

OBU notes that the Democratic Party is bankrupt–that is, intellectually and ethically… they have plenty of cash and that's all they want and appeal for. And OBU contends that MoveOn is likewise useless with its endless petitions and outrages and appeals for yet more money.

These organizations exist. How can they be OBU?

OBU is the personal exchange of tongues, OBU is shared food, OBU is feeling good together, OBU is arguing hard questions, OBU is insistent, OBU is the actual allotment of time, OBU is new songs for the movement, OBU is poetry that scatters when you read, then reassembles, differently, behind your eyes, OBU is the urgency of play the way children play as they do a project, OBU is the return to privacy but then the coming back out from privacy, OBU is art but also something not art, OBU is politics but not always politics, OBU is the personal relationship and the slow accretion of relationships, OBU is the war of accretion, OBU is care searching for an economy of scale.

OBU is person to person, person by person. But the personal is too slow.

OBU is the speed of the digital, the depth of the personal.

OBU is searching for its code and searching for its womb.

OBU yearns to exist, even as it does not exist.

But OBU continuously exists in its yearning.

OBU Manifesto #13

OBU REALIZES THAT MOST OF THE TIME, NOBODY IS HOME.

OBU will soon be blasting out of the probable, out of the possible, out of the plausible.

But when you knock on the door, chances are that nobody is home.

The process could be quite painful. There are powerful G-Forces in the breakaway escape from gravity, in pushing through the thin envelope of atmosphere.

But when you get there, there will in all likelihood be nobody home.

Who did you talk to, OBU? Oh, a couple of people. And what did they say? They seemed sympathetic. Did they fill out the survey? Yeah, part of it. Are they on for the Contra-Trumpista event? Maybe; got to get back to them.

The process could be quite inertial. It may feel like nothing.

The best thing happening right now, OBU suspects grimly, is Alec Baldwin doing his Trump imitation on *Saturday Night Live*.

The old divisions of the Left, OBU notes, are opening up again in force. More taste! Less filling! Is it a breath mint or a candy mint? Is the fundamental oppression race or class? Is our primary enemy capital or white supremacy? Or wait, isn't there anyone there to say "patriarchy"? Is feminism so far out of style? And then there's the very strange and disturbing class/race/public/private rift over charter schools, in which the white bourgeois professional class Leftists hate charter schools and significant numbers of working class African Americans are drawn to them—and hate teachers unions. Yes, that's happening too.

Clearly, no one is home.

OBU has *a lot* of work to do just to get the Left to achieve some solidarity among all its branches.

OBU says, yes, it's complicated, but it's really not impossible to get a handle on.

OBU says, listen, ok? Respect other people's opinions and experiences.

OBU is respect for those divergences. OBU is maintaining a certain distance from one's own experiences and opinions. The differences with one's allies, with those who should be one's allies, are the most painful and infuriating. One thinks, Oh really, so that's the best you can come up with? We're supposed to go into the battle with capital armed with *that* set of analyses and tactics?! Bunch of fucking useless morons. No-no-no... dial that back. It's not like one's own methods and analyses are exactly turning the tide.

The Movement to be must be able to organize and especially in areas outside the Blue Urban Bubbles (the BUBS). It must be able to play in the Red Zones and come away with some TD's, not just settle for field goals. Well, ok, if it's 4th and 5, take the 3. Come away with something.

And how is this to be done and who is going to do it? It can be done through religious organizations. If there are anti-oligarchy, OBUist congregations in the BUBs, they have denominational fellows in or near the Red Zones. Strengthen those relationships. Organize exchanges. Make cultures of solidarity and justice come into being across the country.

And the unions are national. Even where they are weak, they still have some presence, or have the resources to create some. It may not be possible to organize workplaces under present circumstances in Red Zones. But unions can work as community organizing units. They can help the churches and other community groups. They can work to change the ideological climate.

For that is what is most needed, OBU thinks: to change the ideological climate. Serious conversations need to be started in lots of Southern, midwestern, western towns; in churches, PTA's, VFW chapters and VA facilities, town council meetings,. We will not necessarily "win" these conversations, not necessarily convert the people we talk to in one conversation or in ten. But we plant the seed of understanding, of empathy for others, of better economic understanding, of historical knowledge, of knowing other people better.

OBU suggests that the organizers always be in pairs and of two races and/or genders. Black, white, Latino, men, women, queer, straight, Christian, Muslim, Jewish, of different classes and levels of education. When the Red Zone family opens its door, it won't just be talking *about* various "others," it will be talking *with* them–that is, with us; and gradually they will see, with themselves.

This is assuming that someone will be home.

OBU Manifesto #14

OBU is One Big Union

OBU is Oligarchy Busters United

OBU observes that Trump is so astonishingly brazen. The fact that he's rude is part of his appeal. He's not polite, judicious, discrete, kinder or gentler. He's a jerk and a clown and he has boatloads of money and the boats to put it in. He doesn't take shit and he doesn't give a shit, and he's all out in the open. All of you polite, liberal, pc jerkoffs and losers–Trump welcomes your contempt. Bring it on, he says. I can dish it back stronger than you can deliver it. Who wouldn't want to be like that? The clown is now king; the Lord of Misrule rules. How can you blame him for being authoritarian? Trump doesn't even realize that the U.S. isn't a monarchy.

If someone is your enemy, OBU observes, you should welcome them as your enemy. Out of that real struggle, some kind of truth will emerge. If you're afraid of that truth, then don't acknowledge your enemy as an enemy. The conflict will still take place, but without your participation. You will lose, or perhaps there will be a stalemate. But no truth will emerge; or whatever emerges will be unreadable.

What are you afraid of?

Are you afraid the majority of people will be against you? Are you afraid that 40% of the people will be against you? Are you afraid of violence? Are you afraid of confrontation?

Don't kill, says OBU. Defend yourself. But once killing starts, as OBU reads the historical documents, it is hard to turn back.

Always be listening, always be talking to those you disagree with–to your enemies. Make violence unnecessary. Be on offense, not defense.

Lower the carbon footprint everywhere. If your taxes are lowered, create escrow accounts for the common good. Defend freedoms of the press– and make the press earn those freedoms. Defend immigrants. Defend teachers. Make public schools important; make them work. Reject the deflection of funding away from public education.

Annihilate euphemisms. "Choice" in education. "Right to Work." Even the famous woman's "Right to Choose"; this is the right to procreate or not, which is not an easy decision, it's not like some consumer "choice." It's a serious thing, it should be taken seriously. The compromise of Roe v. Wade is sensible and should be defended–but it's not about "choice," it's about necessity and judgement, it's about entire contexts of life as each woman lives it.

Defend unions, and insist that unions work for the common good not just for their particular contracts. Unions now face existential threats; it's time for them to conceive of broader visions for why they exist.

What can defeat Trumpism and the Oligarchy that was there before and is still in power? No existing group can do it. The Democratic Party clearly can't do it (and the Democratic Party in truth is the liberal branch of the Oligarchy). Organized labor as it currently exists can't do it. MoveOn can't do it. Common Cause can't do it. Environmentalist groups can't do it. Black Lives Matter can't do it. OBU can't do it.

It will take more than we can imagine; we have to imagine better.

OBU Interlude #2

to actually imagine

    what

        an effective politics would look

   and sound

      like

if it could be brought into being what it would

      be

    what it would be

  what it   would

    if it   could

       While we

   resist

while we resist

    each

     threat

      each

       implementation

      each

  appointment

                                            each

        degradation

                    each

                        curtailment

                            each

                                insult

                                    each devastating

theft and poisoning of the lived-in living world

        while we resist and maybe win a little

            and maybe lose

                            a lot

It might not be

                    such a bad idea

                                to think through

what

        it

                might

                    be

what

        it

            might

                    look like

                    that thing

                    to be thought

OBU Manifesto #15

OBU IS UP! OBU IS IN ACTION!

OBU is at the major international airports. The unconstitutional detentions of non-citizens with valid visas and Green Cards reentering the U.S. is being contested. People are at the airports. Dictatorship and government by whim will not be accepted. OBU is the spirit of not-lying-down for these abuses.

The judge rules in favor of law and against dictatorship.

A Dictator believes he can *dictate*. He must be shown he cannot.

OBU is Jews protecting Muslims and Christians protecting Muslims and Muslims protecting Jews. No one group will allow the others to be oppressed. When the Dictator came for the Muslims, the Jews and Christians and blacks and whites and browns all were there. Nobody said, I am not a Muslim.

The Dictator may have been elected—by a minority with help of a racist, archaic constitutional atavism—but OBU will not allow him to dictate.

This is a day both of shame and of pride.

OBU is in action.

OBU Manifesto #16

The new inflatable junta has now assumed power. The day after its assumption, the gatherings of OBU arose in cities across the world. These gatherings were miraculous. The influxes, effusions, arms, wings, tentacles, claws, teeth, epidermis, organs, hair, fur, feathers, scales, eyes, ears, nostrils, tongues, gyroscopes, barometers, altimeters, pussy-hats, clarinets, alter kockers, meandering effluvia, snare drums, cymbals and trumpets, symbols of strumpets of OBU in the happy procrastinations of filling the thoroughfares of cities and scraping like noisy glaciers toward the citadels of stolen authority... all this was, well, let's say, a good opening gambit.

OBU is pleased to see that, yes, we can do this. We can put, across the country, a million people in the street– two million, three million.

Can we bring 10 million? Could the spirit of OBU produce even a *General Strike*? When will we choose to do this? At what provocation? For what assertion?

And OBU knows that even the most numerous manifestations of popular will and feeling can be ignored. Have been ignored. A million people? That means that 299 million people did not march. Who needs to pay attention to a million? Or two? Or three?

But, ok, OBU thinks, these three million of us–that's our core. Can we increase it? OBU would assume we can. The three million is OBU; it has shown itself. And second, will the multitudes of OBU and its tributaries (whose only "tributes" are courage, intelligence, compassion, commitment, energy, and all the non-marketable forces of life) be ready to assemble at short notice to protect schools, health care facilities, workers and unions, immigrants, minorities threatened by state power, whistleblowers, dissidents, journalists, artists, teachers, rivers, forests, the air, the oceans...?

OBU is One Big Union

Will OBU and its OBU-ite friends who turned out in such numbers for these rallies to oppose the Trumpist misogynocracy also turn out to not *allow* a single public school, public utility, public land to be privatized?

OBU asks, apropos of an earlier comment, what are the relations between a "tribute," a "tributary," and an "attribute"? A "tribute" is a form of praise. One "pays tribute" to a person who has accomplished something significant. But the economic-political metaphor is already present. To "pay tribute" also means to concede certain spoils or rewards of conquest to a conqueror. The payment of tribute is not voluntary; it is coerced. And the "tributary" is the smaller stream that flows into, pays into, contributes to the larger river. Indeed, by the time the river reaches the sea, most of its waters have been obtained through such "tributes." Would we then say that these contributions are what comprise finally its attributes?

OBU's brief research reveals that the common root of these words is the Latin *tribus*, meaning "tribe," which then is refigured as the verb *tribuere,* to assign–specifically, to assign among tribes.

OBU is the tribe of solidarity and democracy; of political and economic justice. The tribe is open to all contributions, attributes, tributes, and tribulations.

OBU locates the porous zones of the sediment. It will overflow the dams and damnings of oligarchy.

Can the tribal be universal? The confluence of tribes? Is every universal by definition a false universal that conceals particular assumptions of power? But then, is there no OBU?

OBU is not a tribe.

OBU is a sediment.

OBU Manifesto #17

What can defeat Trumpism and the Oligarchy that was there before and is still in power? No existing group can do it. The Democratic Party? Organized labor? MoveOn with all its calls and links and petitions? Not likely. Environmentalist groups can't do it. Black Lives Matter can't do it. Immigrants' rights groups can't do it. Common Cause can't do it. If ACORN still existed, it couldn't do it. The ACLU can't do it. Doctors Without Borders can't do it. Lawyers Without Doctors can't do it. Ben and Jerry can't do it.

Every person and organization must seek to understand his/her/its limits, and then seek to go beyond them.

How much time do you have, OBU wants to know? What hours do you have to commit to work, to your family, to the activities that give your life meaning and pleasure? And what do you have to give to working to create the solidarities that will save this country and this planet?

What talents do you have? Can you talk with people? Can you write? Can you walk? How are your knees and hips? Can you make phone calls? Can you tell time? Can you show people how you feel about where this country is going? Do you have a gift for teaching? Are you good at listening? How good are you at failure? Have you ever witnessed shit hitting a fan? What reserves of courage do you have? Are you good at working with people? Are you good at working alone? Do you have the ability to recognize when "push" does actually come to "shove"?

What can you give?

OBU is One Big Union

Everything we need to do now, OBU agrees, we should have done already. We should have stood up for unions–and forced the Democratic Party to do so. We should have gotten serious about climate change. We should have–how can OBU put it–not been so sanctimonious about "diversity," but rather have accelerated real processes of racial integration and cultural interaction and created real environments in which all different ethnic racial gendered geographic religious groups might live, work, and study together. We should have rethought all the standard assumptions about economics, about the need for growth, the imperatives of profit; we should have busted our butts creating a sustainable economy that does not produce material or human waste, that does not produce poverty and environmental devastation as "externalities."

But we didn't, and now here we are.

OBU is Oligarchy Busters United? (So, let's see it).

OBU Manifesto #18

Who can be the messenger or harbinger?

In what medium?

OBU says, we will have a FaceBook page! We will publish a manifesto as an online op-ed in *The New Republic* or *Salon*, maybe get on in *Huff Post*!

OBU will infiltrate the world of Left Avant-Garde poetics and be hailed as an underground masterpiece.

OBU will somehow sneak itself past the sacred arbiters of the *New York Times*.

OBU will hack into CNN, MSNBC and Fox News and deliver its ultimatums of solidarity, decency, and reclaiming the public sphere.

OBU is the archaic torso of Apollo without head or arms or legs that tells you *"You must change your political economy, you must change your systems of assigning value, you must change your style of poetry...* oh, and...

You must change your life.

OBU is Oligarchy Busters United

Conceive it.

Don't tell OBU why this is naive or impossible. Everyone is OBU's midwife and parent. Everyone contributes her/his/their skill, illnesses, genetic mashup, stubbornness, resentment, fatigue, their unleashing of freedom, their vestigial slavery, their wakefulness and their plastic cutlery, and all reserves of hope and love.

Bring it to birth.

And to all the crusty fellows who say, One Big anything is just a monolith, and what we need are free individuals free to exercise their freedom, as if freedom were some pet you need to take out for a walk twice a day or a specific muscle group your personal trainer can help you develop. Well, you've got it wrong. Learn another tune.

And if you crusty fellows feel, after due consideration, that you need to stand with the oligarchy in order to enjoy your freedom in all its fullness and grandeur–like, say, the Grand Canyon after it's been opened to the freedom of mineral extraction—then please do some rethinking, or get out of the way. The solidarities of OBU are coming through.

To be free in the earshot of oppression is to join the oppressor, says OBU.

What does it mean, OBU asks, to be a free human being? And how does one address unfreedom?

"Black Lives Matter," for instance– and they matter in precisely the particular historical and cultural ways that the slogan intends. *Black* lives must be made to matter, must be given value, because of the histories of violence and violation directed against the lives of black people. This is not, as they say, rocket science–although the heroines of *Hidden Figures* could have given us some accurate algorithms for our national orbital reentry.

But if black lives are to matter, then black *livelihoods* must matter just as profoundly. Black people must live and make a living. They must not be killed, and they must flourish, prosper, and thrive. They must *live*—as black people, as people, as descendants and cultural heirs of Africans, and as Americans.

Racial justice and economic justice–and the political power required to bring these about–none of these are separate, OBU believes. All are entwined. Freedom, for real, cannot exist until these goals are accomplished.

OBU is One Big Union

OBU Manifesto #19

THE MOVEMENT IS THE SUM OF ALL MOVEMENTS (THOUGH IT DOESN'T YET exist). The movement is the empty space between the movements. The movement is the dark matter that allows all that we see to cohere.

OBU is a gravitational attraction.

OBU is all the people who go from meeting to meeting trying to find the group whose focus corresponds most closely to their own.

OBU is the realization that they will never find it.

And every night and morning, they'll complain, oh those guys, they don't know how to organize and those guys, they don't have any real vision, and those over there, they're just lobbyists and fundraisers, and those guys don't know the Democratic Party is bankrupt, and those ones don't admit that 3rd parties brought us Bush II and Trump, and over there they only think about the narrow interests of organized labor, but over there they don't realize that without organized labor there is no movement, and those guys are completely clueless about race, and those guys think the whole thing is always about race and get all bent out of shape with everyone else, and those twits are a bunch of old hippie peacenik dimwits, and over there it's the reality-challenged millennial dopes, and this contingent is so self-righteous they have golden rose stems up their asses, and then there's those guys that couldn't get three ten-year olds to march down a street for free ice cream.

OBU IS OXYMORONIC BALLOONS UNTETHERED

Face it, OBU concludes, the Left is shot. Every single tiny facet of it is ineffectual, and every facet thinks that every other facet is *more* ineffectual.

But, then we pulled off those Women's Marches– 3 million people across the country (just about the number by which Hilary *won* the election). That was amazing, there's no getting around it. That was a *demonstration*. That was a beginning for OBU.

And that is important to remember, is it not? Hilary *lost* by 60,000 in Wisconsin, Michigan, and Pennsylvania, but she *won* by 3,000,000 in the whole country.

OBU needs never to lose sight of that fact, of that reality. She's a liberal, globalist, technocrat with close ties to the financial industry. But she's not a racist or sexist, and she's not a pathological narcissist and she's not delusional. Three million more liberal, tolerant, at least somewhat cosmopolitan people voted for her than frightened, angry, variously xenophobic, intolerant people voted for DT.

OBU acknowledges that this fact should give us hope.

On the other hand, OBU reasons, let's say Hilary won... How would we assimilate the fact that 48 or 49% of the electorate voted for Trump? One would feel relieved Hilary won, but not feel a substantial amount of hope.

OBU would still be necessary if Hilary had won.

OBU is Oligarchy Busters United, and don't forget it!

There is no mistaking what is surrounding us. It is very dark. The darkness is not opaque. Objects are more visible than ever. Social forces are vivid, they are not abstract. Never before, OBU remarks, in the lives of the living, have we seen in this country, on this scale, such love of darkness, such mad embrace of the wind's teeth, the insult, the threat, the love of force.

OBU also recognizes that African Americans may question that assertion... *"Never before....????"* Well, ok, so now that darkness is more widely visible and more broadly directed; maybe more complicated, its economic components also more exposed. If we weren't together before, let's make sure we're together now.

OBU does not hate hatred. OBU fights hatred.

OBU fights to overcome and defeat hatred at every lattice, tree trunk, construction site, city council meeting, baseball game, tree root, retail outlet, leaf and branch, music practice room, union hall, presidential inauguration, church, temple, mosque, synagogue, park, amber wave of grain, crevice and doorknob. OBU will raise the blinds, it will reason with its interlocutors, it will appeal to the fellow-feeling of intelligent sentient beings, it will shove aside those who will not reason or empathize–get out of the way and let someone with more reason and fellow-feeling come forward!–OBU will defend itself and defend those who are attacked.

OBU wishes the passionate feelings of love to be unrestrained. OBU will carefully monitor the passions that lead toward violence. Once the force of righteous vengeance is set free, it is very difficult to call back. And what vengeance, after all, is not called "righteous"?

OBU continues.

OBU is One Big Union

OBU Manifesto #20

OBU IS OF THE OPINION THAT TO HAVE A POLITICAL OPINION AT THIS MOMENT IS pretty trivial. We all had plenty of opinions before the election. And now we have pretty much the same ones, except now they're **ALL IN BOLD CAPS WITH MULTIPLE EXCLAMATION POINTS!!!!!!**

BUT, it is also trivial to be ironic–not in the sense in which irony was purportedly "dead" after 9/11—but in that irony is now just another scripted response to the political crisis. Those tempermentally tending toward irony will, naturally, be ironic. Those without irony will still be without irony.

AND to think one knows what **TO DO** is obviously delusional.

AND to bemoan that one does not know *what to do* is redundant.

AND to fulminate is obvious. And to identify the useless self-indulgent hand-wringing and blaming the Left (or the Center) of one's friends and allies is always tempting, but just as useless. We failed, ok. And we've been failing for the past eight years, don't forget that. We failed in 2010 and 2014. We allowed the Tea Party to come into being unopposed. We allowed racial antagonism and xenophobia to entwine themselves with economic grievances–we saw this and did nothing to disentangle them. This has been the Right Wing/Republican strategy since 1965 and we still have no answer for it.

OBU IS STILL ONE BIG UNION, OR ASPIRES TO BE...

OBU says, how the fuck is this possible?

As previously mentioned, however, to fulminate is obvious.

And **OBU** is still **O**ligarchy **B**usters **U**nited
(and vibrant fulmination may be a necessary step)

OBU does not believe that the inevitable endgame of this conflict is civil war. OBU acknowledges that the reason for this may be that the Left and liberals simply lack the courage to fight and so the Right will win without fighting. They will win through voter suppression, truth and reality suppression, and the continued convincing of white middle and working classes that they are an oppressed minority (all the while further impoverishing them so that they will resent other races all the more).

OBU Manifesto #21

WE MUST REIMAGINE OURSELVES AS THE MAKERS OF OUR WORLD.

To write a poem means to imagine the person capable of writing that poem. Usually that person isn't "you" as you currently exist.

OBU does not "currently exist"; and yet these documents affirming it are real.

Imagining OBU: If OBU had organs of language and expression, what would it say? If it had sensory organs, what would it see and hear and feel and taste. If it had a mind, what would be the contents of its consciousness? Or of its many consciousnesses?

If it had wheels...

Would it be our grandmother?

Things seem so simple until they're not. OBU hears, Give everyone a voucher so they can send their kids to a school that doesn't have unions– and that's called "choice." If you pay lower taxes, you imagine you don't need higher wages. If you buy things cheap at Walmart, well then no worries if you have to work there too. If the problem is the government and its taxes and regulations, will the company keep the air and water clean and the workplace safe? If the problem is the unions, will you trust yourself to the market?

What's your value, says OBU? What are you worth? When you boldly address the corporation and tell them you are indispensable, what does HR reply to you. When, by yourself, you proudly, individually and autonomously proclaim your worth and demand your recompense and ask really no more than a wage that will let you feed your family, make a car payment, send a kid to college maybe (maybe!?), what will the company say to you?

The market will determine your value, it's nothing personal that you will have no health insurance or pension, that you can't afford healthy food, that when you become sick or your car breaks down you lose your dwelling.

Can we reimagine ourselves as the makers of our world?

OBU is One Big Union

The heroic entrepreneurs and the great powers of finance are crushing working people into the ground and the reason is simple: because they don't need them.

"Surplus labor," OBU observes, has always been a necessary feature of capitalism, a means of coping with the ups and downs of demand and a way to keep wages under control. But now nearly all labor is surplus, from college faculty to health care to manufacturing to clerical work to agriculture to fast food and retail... It's all, "we'll call you when we need you." And everyone is so eager to cooperate: "Yes, yes, please call us, we'll do whatever you ask for whatever you'll pay us!! (It's only our lives that depend on it)."

OBU is Oligarchy Busters United

OBU is the power of each person to reject and resist his market value.

This must be understood by each person individually. But it can only be acted on collectively, for the public must be reclaimed from the private, for not everything has a price and not every value can be expressed in dollars, and we breathe the same air, our bodies have the same pleasures and ailments, our children's minds have the same curiosity, we share the love of beauty, of humor, of time to relax, of food that tastes good and makes us strong, of open space, of a clean, warm home with food in the fridge and some vodka in the freezer, of work that pays a fair wage and accomplishes something meaningful. We share all these loves and dreams in common. These are public goods. These are for everyone.

Whenever and wherever some people enjoy these public goods and others do not; when some people regard these public goods as their private earnings and entitlements and many, many others possess but a fraction, in these cases we know a crime is being committed. We are witnesses to a crime; and if we do nothing, we are parties to that crime.

OBU Interlude #3

THE SADDEST THING IN THE WORLD IS JOY. WHY IS THAT?

We're going to beat them, we know this, don't we?

The dictator is going to lose. And then we'll feel joy.

We will not let another life be wasted.

We will live for others and live for ourselves

and the residue of our lives will be joy

and the waste products of our economy will be beauty

and excesses of love for which we have insufficient objects.

And no one will be crushed. And all abilities will be cherished.

We will cherish the ability to make amazing clear intricate poems

and the ability to heal, the ability to do difficult math and to program computers,

the ability to care for children, the ability to coordinate and lead a manufacturing process,

the ability to make music of all kinds, the ability to care for old people,

the ability to make movies, the ability to direct an agency that is compassionate

and effective, the ability to run a home, the abilities to build and to repair,

the wonderful capacity for friendship, the careful patient skill and love needed to bring up children, the ability to cook, the ability to brew beer,

skill at letting things grow.

Generosity, humor, sympathy, organization, articulateness,

affection, grace, nonverbal physical communication, strength

and inevitable human weakness... all these will be cherished.

But the ability to lie and the ability to wield power over others, and the ability to make deals that only benefit oneself and the ability

to strategize for personal gain and the ability to throw people away

like garbage and the ability to manufacture garbage in all forms and materials

and to create an economy whose entire logic is the separation of gold from shit,

the hoarding and flaunting of one the expulsion of the other across the social and eco-systems –

these abilities will no longer be known or understood. Historical records will tell of them,

and we will read those stories and be more bewildered than repulsed.

Our world will flow around axes of joy and love and freedom and imagination.

The eroticism of domination and subservience will be known only

in the cultural artefacts of the past.

No one will worship power.

We will feel in ourselves the joy that now we experience mainly across

the mediations of art, in the movies and in songs.

What we now feel through them we will feel on our own and through each other, all of us, young and old.

We will not be crushed by poverty or by how people look at us.

We will participate in the civic world, we will make together the decisions

that most affect our lives, we will have fine schools taught by compassionate, brilliant teachers, and everyone will teach and learn.

Work will not be oppression. Leisure will not be mindless escape. Love will be full, without reserve or shame.

Our full lives, minds, and hearts will be engaged in our every endeavor.

The feeling of every moment will be a feeling of eternity.

The sense of joy will be the shadow just passing always into your field.

It's only now that the saddest thing in the world is joy.

OBU Manifesto #22

OBU IS THE COLLECTIVE PREHENSILE TAIL OF THE FUTURE. OBU IS THE OPPOSABLE thumb and shift of the pelvic alignment that allow for better grasping and broader perspectives. OBU might be a slight but perceptible enlargement of unknown regions of the cortex that will facilitate greater powers of sympathy, increased moral courage, a slight decrease in modes of physical courage (which will thereafter be regarded as forms of folly, cruelty, and recklessness), and more astonishing capacities for artistic creation and enhanced, interpersonal rationality.

OBU is not "post-human."

OBU is *posit-human*. We don't have it yet, but it's there. There's nothing comes after except nothing.

Well, all right, OBU acknowledges. Old Octavia Butler has a point–maybe we're drastically misconfigured. We need another gender and different forms of sexuality, we need to rewire our destructive leanings toward hierarchy–we need to interbreed with an alien species that can mend our homicidal rough edges; or, as in Marge Piercy's utopia, we need to separate sexual relations from child-rearing, eliminate live birth, let men lactate, and choose leaders by lottery; or, as in Margaret Atwood's post-apocalyptic glummering, delink procreation and sexuality from all symbolic overlays and underpinnings; females will go into heat, they and males will fuck, they'll birth the babes, they'll care for them and let them go when mature... and all this without fantasy, property, or literature.

According to some, all culture–that is, all symbolic-social achievements beyond the needs of subsistence, at least since the start of agriculture and settled, urban society–all is based, essentially, on slavery in some form. Call it what you like; some form of subservience. One class enjoys and does the bulk of cultural creation and the enjoyment of that creation; other classes labor so that the higher class can create and enjoy. Whatever the terminology, it boils down to forms of slavery. In any society, how many people can simply... *stop working*? And for whom are they working? For those who have more than they, for those who have power over them. The power consists in the most immediate way in making them work. The freedom anyone in the "working classes" has is the freedom to starve.

OBU is One Big Union

"By the sweat of your brow shall you eat your bread," etc., says one of the earliest manifestos of the ruling class– a very interesting manifesto in that it is also, at the same time, a manifesto for liberation.

This is not really so surprising, OBU considers. The need to work is presented as simple realism. The question, even from this earliest moment, is who receives the fruit of the labor? Who gets the first cut, and who gets whatever is left over after all other expenses are met? Whose payment and subsistence detract from the real purpose of the economy– which is the leisure of the rulers?

Leisure, pleasure, meaning, beauty, OBU exhales, "the finer things" as they used to be called. These are the products and goals to which all others yield. All the mines and plantations and factories and retail outlets and healthcare empires and universities and investment banks, and all the public schools that train the workers and the cheap, poisonous food available to all (in the developed [sic] world), all the extractive industries, all the "externalities" that cover the planet with filth (except the enclaves of the wealthy), and all the force of the state, the violence threatened and the violence inflicted... What is all this mess and violence? The entire economy, public and private, is one great Externality continually produced so that a fittingly comfortable life can be enjoyed by the Few.

Oligarchy is the rule of the few. This is their world. The rest of us just work here.

Their lives are comfortable and meaningful. Luxury, of course, is relative. Some crave luxury, some prefer just to live in comfort. Unashamed luxury is sometimes in style, sometimes not. Let's say beauty and meaning are the jewels on the crown of oligarchy. Thus, the system justifies itself, for the values of the affluent are obviously superior to the values of the poor: their sports, their pathetic lotteries, their petty crimes, their unsavory gangs, their pathetic imitations of the styles of the rich, their incomprehensible countercultures which are quickly appropriated by capital, their envious worship of wealth, their addictions and health problems and poor diets, their illiteracy, their short life-spans, their poor taste and shopping habits.

OBU IS OLIGARCHY BUSTERS UNITED

OBU Manifesto #23

OBU SAYS, IT'S TIME TO GET OVER IT.

And OBU does not mean, it's time to get over the (electoral college) election of The Donald. No, that is not to be gotten over; that's to be fought at every point. That will not be *gotten over* as long as the United States has any existence.

It's time to get over the divisions within the Resistance, the divisions within OBU. The white liberal types need to get over the black people being mad at them for showing up for big (mostly) white demonstrations when they weren't there for Black Lives Matter events. And white people, some of them, do need to get over the idea that *they* uniquely understand the *big picture*, while other groups only understand their particular viewpoints. It's not true; get over it.

But black people need to get over it too. Oppression in America has many forms. Black anger is justified and necessary; but at a certain point, figure out what alliances and solidarities need to be made, and make them.

And yes, ok, this is a certain portion of OBU talking, and fuck OBU! Right. Now, let's proceed.

And all the straight cis-gender people need to get over being upset at being castigated by the queer trans people for not being sufficiently down with defending and celebrating queer trans lives and identities. And the queer trans people need to get over the straight cis-gender people not being attuned enough to the realities of their lives. Everybody's got problems. That's actually true.

Fuck OBU from both sides and out from the center! Yes, ok, now let's proceed.

The point, OBU observes, is that *here we are now*. We're all here. This is real. We're not going to wake up out of it. And the *"WE"* is real. The historical situation is real, and the historical subject–first person plural–is real. HERE–WE–ARE–NOW.

OBU asks, are you somewhere else, and where might that be?

OBU IS, AND REMAINS, ONE BIG UNION

So, it's time to get over it, whatever your particular "it" happens to be. Whoever you resent, for whatever valid or questionable historical and experiential reasons; whoever is in your face, and you want them out of your face; whoever is full of their self-righteous bullshit; whoever has said they're your friend and then walked away when it mattered; whoever was with you mainly to make themselves feel good; whoever thinks their struggle is the central struggle or the only struggle... It's all there, it's all happened. And it will keep happening, no doubt about it.

OBU knows that alliances are not gatherings of clones. And alliances are not military or corporate command structures where everyone follows the orders of their superiors or of the central committee.

OBU IS OLIGARCHY BUSTERS UNITED

OBU knows that many times we're going to get into it and get fractious. Fighting oligarchy and fighting for the rule of the many, not the few, means dealing with racism, xenophobia, gender injustices of all sorts, corporate power, environmental destruction, energy policy, health care, workers' rights, the very role of work, disability, immigration... All of these need to be addressed, and at every moment the main emphases may shift and shift again. But, OBU contends, this is not a checklist, this is not a situation where each "interest group" solely advances their own interests, and we are "diverse," yet not genuinely united. All these struggles are one struggle. If we don't see that yet, then we need to think some more and conceptualize it so that we see it.

OBU does not see the organizational model as one of "intersectionality." OBU understands the rationale–the sense that notions of "solidarity" subsume minority concerns, especially of race and gender, under a monovocal false universal that ends up male and white.... Yes, precisely. But OBU insists that solidarity is the method that will win, that must win. Solidarity is only real when it is learned and earned, when it is achieved, which means, when it is in-process; solidarity is the hand as it is extended and when it grasps the other hand; it is words exchanged as they are exchanged, in that act of exchange; solidarity is actions taken together; compromises reached; risks taken together.

Intersectionality is vapid and abstract. Get in the room together, OBU suggests, and figure it out. "Intersections" are for lines and roads.

If whatever leadership evolves does not have people of different races, classes, genders, educational levels, then we're doing something wrong. But don't flip out... Try again. Get it right. Get together with good, committed, bright people from different places who know how to work with other people. Why should that be so hard?

OBU acknowledges it's easy to say that everyone is included. It's difficult to actually achieve that goal.

OBU Manifesto #24

OBU ASKS, SO, IS THE WORLD COMING TO AN END?

Donald Trump seems to think so. America is in a state of "carnage," its cities are in ruins, federal troops have been sent to occupy Chicago. Mad Max has bought a controlling interest in Nascar. We're running out of fuel; we need that Arctic oil and we need the pipelines to bring it in. We need those construction jobs for the white men so that they don't OD on meth and have to pawn their AK-47s and camo fatigues and have to miss militia target practice and the revolution against Obamacare fizzles out as Republican legislators realize they don't know how to replace it.

So, is the world coming to an end?

As soon as North Korea gets its ICBM correctly targeted at Los Angeles and Iran gets its missiles straight for Tel Aviv and Russia takes over Latvia directing its attack from a secret hacker site in Coney Island and Maylasia declares martial law and the Philippines demands reparations for a war we don't remember we fought and Donald Trump opens a Trump Casino in Jordan to the delight of Israelis and Palestinians alike.

And the penultimate glacier melts and the contours of the continents shift and all our present coastlines and coastal cities are underwater. And Tanzania opens a ski resort on Kilimanjaro having purchased artificial snow machines with the last of its foreign currency. And the latest bird flu virus mutates to airborn communicability and the last antibiotic loses its efficacy. And there is still no such thing as zombies, but contagious refugees of climate and disease now are crossing all borders and somehow boring through every barrier, there is no longer any containment. And the Dow hits 35,000 as droughts destroy the American wheat and soy crops. Many fortunes will be made investing in cremation equipment. And the last union member in the last state not to have "right to work" laws refuses to pay her dues. Her contract does not include burial benefits. And the union has no bank account in which to deposit the dues.

OBU asks, is the world coming to an end?

Not yet, not yet, we're not ready yet... The interstellar space craft with a million suspended animation pods has not been completed. It cannot be that the earth's rulers will have to perish here with the rest of us. But wait, they are preparing their Habitable Zones across the still-fertile latitudes; with advanced longevity technologies they will get to live to see everyone else die, and then they will cleanse the depopulated planet, and culture and benevolence will abound. Imagine the histories they will write of those heroic, pioneering days!

OBU WAS ONCE ONE BIG UNION

But it failed. It broke into pieces.

OBU WAS ONCE OLIGARCHY BUSTERS UNITED

But it shattered against the concentrated power of wealth united and determined to preserve itself, even at the price of ending the world.

(Anti-) OBU Manifesto (#25)

OBU IN *ReversoVerse*. It's Alt-World U-Verse InVerse. Slides in slushy swerves from version to inversion. Come on, let's get real, that news is fake. No, your news is fake; no, your news is fake. Your nose is fake! And that's a fake noose. Nyeah, nyeah, nyeah! I'd say the dude is fat. The dude is not fat. I read a report said the dude is fat. The report is biased, the report is liberal. I saw the dude stand on a scale, weighed 400 pounds, was hacking your email. He could have been a Russian, he could have been wearing a bulky sweater, and that wasn't a scale. The scale was in kilos he was selling dope, it's hidden in his silicon ManBoobs.

Obama didn't write the books he wrote, OBU hears, but who cares, who would read them. The Pope voted for Trump–not voter fraud, he's infallible although he's a Catholic. Hilary personally raped campaign staff, if you can call that rape, with her own broomstick, not that she can actually fly, she's actually a terrible witch, for a witch. The pizza Sex-gate thing was actually about trading pizzas for Obama Care premiums and deductibles. The Republicans are so much more the Party for civil rights because of Lincoln of course, but also because more Republicans resisted LBJ's racist repression to vote for civil rights legislation, and the problem today really is that black people don't know how good they have it and want to take away the rights of white people. It's become a nation of so-called victims with the blacks and the gays and the Hispanics, everybody thinks somebody owes them something. Well guess what. No white person ever got anything for free. It you don't believe it, it's written down right there on my rectum and you can take a look. Kiss me if I'm wrong.

OBU does not want to exaggerate, but this is what he got transmitted on his new VR goggles, got it all in 3D Sensurround, amazing effect, luckily the interactive mode wasn't hooked in or OBU would have gotten its collective ass kicked and its New Solidarity completely shit all over.

OBU sees good Episcopalian gentlemen in clerical collars quoting the *National Enquirer*. You know that Don Drysdale and Tommy Lasorda both were killed by Sandy Koufax after they stopped him from doing a human sacrifice at his secret Passover feast. But the shameful part was that Mike Piazza was his assistant. And! Human sacrifice for Jewish festivals *is* covered by Obamacare.

OBU is made to understand that Sharia Law is actually in effect in three states–Pennsylvania, Michigan, and Kansas. Cutting off people's hands is not such a bad idea. Covering up women, well, each to his own, personally OBU likes to see a little skin now and again, keeps him feelin' peppy although OBU is very much in favor of strict sexual morality. Biggest problem is the price of meat what with that Halal thing they got goin'. And if OBU's got to eat another goddamn falafel, it's going to move on back to Oklahoma.

The law of the Land is "take what you can get." Is there some other law you'd prefer? I mean that in a legal sense, in the sense of everyone has the right to *buy* what they can *afford*. And everyone has a right to *borrow* at a rate of interest deemed profitable by the lender in order to buy what they *can't* afford. This used to be called "indenture" and in our textbooks, it's considered a step above slavery–temporary slavery for white people. But now it's back, a valued part of the economic system.

The market is good for everything, OBU understands; it's good for what ails you, it delivers the goods and gives you freedom if you've got the jack to get in the game, if you've got the goods. It's good.

And the most delicious part of the market, of course, is the universal market of sexual desire, at least for men; OBU has got to do a bit more research to see how it works for women.

OBU IS, YEAH BABY!

OBU Manifesto #26

The questioning of "we" is legitimate, OBU acknowledges. Who, after all, is "we"? If all of "us" are not speaking simultaneously and unanimously, then who is it that is speaking for "us"?And how do "we" know that the rest of "us," who are not speaking, are really part of the "we"? "Solidarity," sure– of Whom with What?

Many Left movements, OBU notices, place great value on the "I" and his or her story. Individuals whose lives and stories have been devalued and dismissed are encouraged to give testimony–to tell the story of who they are, how they live, what they aspire to. In speaking, they show their value, and they show their ability to wield power. This is of tremendous importance. It is also assumed that in speaking for themselves, these individuals speak also for their particular demographic categories. They speak for people of color, for women, for queers, for the disabled, for immigrants, for Latino/as. They say, this is what happened to me, to those like me. These powerful stories should be told and heard. For someone who had not previously been listened to now to be listened to is a powerful political event. This is *my* story. And in this accretion of "I"s will come an association full of the drive toward justice and power.

OBU is Oligarchy Busters United

But who creates the "we"? If there is to be a "we"? The individuals in this ceremony provide their own "I"s. Only the leaders, it seems, are equipped to extrapolate the "we" in which real power resides. The "we," in these cases, OBU submits, is a kind of administrative fiction. The "I" must be articulated and maintained, each "I" in its unique integrity, and also (though OBU senses, more dubiously) in its synechdocal relation to its demographic constituency. But the "I" also, like an atom with complex electron fields, must have the ability to bond and create powerful social substances which can then form further bonds. If we are atoms, we must be carbon atoms whose astonishing ability to link and merge creates all life.

The single atom: the testimony, the anecdote. But how do we create the we... the compound and synthesis, the full drama, the novel, the deep presentation and analysis in narrative and dialogue?

OBU is One Big Union

But is OBU's lament just a cry for new forms of meaningful wheeze, or its sense of solidarity just amorphous porousness and solubility that can be ladled into tankards of any shape? Solidarity is easy for liquids and gases and for schools of fish or colonies of insects or coral. But for a species that puts its eggs on its shoulders and whose motto is the Latin inscription for "feckless," whose divination rod is always double–one branch pointing up, the other pointing down–it's hard to trust the gut that says, "love" or even "affinity" when the rumble sounds just as much like "hunger."

But yet, but still, the larger "we" is there, it exists, can exist, it is inhabitable, capacious, adjustable. Large numbers of "I"s can venture in and it will fit them, and they will not lose their integrity, they will not lose their kindness or openness toward those not wrapped in the garment. They will understand that the world is to be held in common–not every part of it, please, don't be ridiculous, at least at this point. There will still be countries and property (though one can imagine otherwise?). But they will understand that the goods of the world, the things that are necessary for life–for biological, cultural and political life; for lives of feeling and happiness; the goods of nature and of art; of oceans and seasons; the goodness of health; of food, air, water; and the goods of meaning, the goods of lives lived well–that these must be goods for everyone, or they have no importance at all.

Solidarity–the meaningful "we"s–OBU asserts, is the knowledge and determination that the age of slavery is finally over, will finally be over. The age of slavery is all of human history. Human history is the history of dominant groups ruling subservient groups, of privileged, powerful classes living lives of absolute or relative ease owing to the work of laboring classes. All other histories, as truly great, remarkable, and illustrious as they are, endure within this history–the history of slavery.

74

We–yes, we–will imagine this solidarity and will achieve it... "so much life and never! And so many years, and always, much always, always, always!"

OBU is [___]

OBU Manifesto #27

THE GOODS OF THE WORLD ARE BEING STOLEN, MORE OR LESS QUICKLY, MORE AND more quickly. They are collected as rents, paid out as capital gains and dividends and interest, extracted from the earth and sea, extracted from the bodies that work, mined from the minds, extracted and skimmed off the top of the budget cuts that destroy public schools, libraries, parks, universities, cultural institutions, affordable housing, food for the hungry.

The goods of the world are being stolen and the earth itself is being stolen.

The plentitude of life is being destroyed for convenience and profit, or carelessly as an "externality" of the economic system. Its genetic stuff is colonized and marketed as millions of unmarketable species are made extinct.

OBU asks, do you doubt this? Is this news?

Is it imprudent to say that the world is now run by enormous criminal cartels called nations and corporations? Is it paranoid to say this? Is it tactically unhelpful? Or shall we say that such a statement works as a kind of analogy or metaphor. "It is *as if* the world were now run..." etc.

Shall we say, OBU suggests, that the current world order is not *actually* a set of competitive but interlocking criminal cartels... It just *resembles* a set of criminal cartels in significant ways.

These ways include:

–Actions strictly in the interest of one's own gang.

–Willingness to use violence to advance those interests.

–Carelessness with regard to collateral damage (to people or [others'!]

property) or the creation of waste and "externalities."

–Patronage and rewards to those who are loyal.

–Punishments for those who rebel.

–Maintenance of an armed force to maintain order.

–Maintaining basic levels of distribution of goods and services.

–Maintaining basic educational and informational systems that inculcate belief in and loyalty to the cartel.

–Maintaining certain cultural and legal norms to create the impression of legitimacy.

–Retaining also the prerogative of acting arbitrarily when deemed necessary.

OBU is Oligarchy Busters United

OBU is

never without debt

never without anger.

OBU does not promise freedom.

OBU does not promise happiness or clarity of mind.

OBU cannot release a heart from anguish.

OBU is the debt of the perpetual imperative, the thing that must be done because it is the thing that ought to be done, and so it must be done.

OBU is the debt that cannot be paid back.

One Big Union

OBU is the obvious thing.

OBU is the reminder, the reminiscence, the remainder. OBU is the insistent tweak, the thing just out of vision, out of focus. And you say, there was something I was thinking of, what was it? And after you've thought of everything else, the thing that's there, in some form, the thing you don't recognize, but are sure you've seen before, is OBU.

OBU does not make all things new. OBU does not balance its accounts.

Debt is always a matter of excess, of obligation that can only partly be met, not a matter of making things square and even.

Someone destroys a wetland or a rain forest, or someone causes a chronic and ultimately fatal disease. They pay damages, let's say. They may satisfy the law, but they do not satisfy the debt.

OBU asks, When you steal what cannot be replaced, what do you owe?

OBU Manifesto #28

In the OBU future, there will be great practical and moral improvements.

People will be better drivers. Why? Because they will be more patient and pay closer attention to what it going on around them. They will have greater respect and empathy for others. They will check their mirrors and their blind spots.

People will be better drivers also because there will be less traffic, more extensive and effective public transportation, better maintained roads. More people will live close their jobs and closer to their families.

It may be, of course, that most cars in the OBU future will be self-driving. In this case, most people will be worse drivers because they won't know how to drive. This may or may not be a good thing. If the self-driving cars are electric and actually don't crash, then presumably it will be a good thing. But in the OBU future, these cars will be designed for short distance, local driving. For longer trips, they will take you to the train station. In the OBU future, trains will be inexpensive and delightful.

In the OBU future, there will be more parties. There will be more occasions for real contact and enjoyment among different groups of people. There will be more music and dancing. There will also be quiet areas for conversation.

In the OBU future, a solution will be found for the problem of standing at a party holding a drink in one hand, a plate of food in the other, and trying to eat something from the plate. In the present, corrupt age, this is not possible.

In the OBU future, people will have more and more various friends. There will also be more fun things to do and more time to do fun things.

In the OBU future, friends, colleagues, and comrades will talk about important things with each other. The condition of the polity, the power and justice of some conceivable or inconceivable deity, the nature of art and of love, the nature of aging and death, the mysterious qualities of sex, what do we really mean by "education," what really are the obligations of citizenship, what does it take to build a movement for justice?–all these will be typical and frequent topics of conversation. (We may also talk about sports, if we really want to... "How 'bout those Mets?! Great staff if they stay healthy!").

OBU is One Big Union

In the OBU future, more people will play musical instruments and take part in dramatic productions. More people will play sports; fewer people will watch other people play them. More people will do math problems for fun. More people will keep up with the latest scientific discoveries. More people will understand basic physics, chemistry, and biology. Video games will be just really passe. OBU would pose the question, what does "interactive" really mean? In what sense is actually doing something with your body not interactive? In what sense is reading not interactive?

In the OBU future, people will wake the fuck up.

In the OBU future, there will be more occasions for solitude.

In the OBU future, the food industry will be utterly reconfigured. The barbarous destructive wasteful poisonous planet-destroying exploitative oppressive and cruel industrial meat industry will have been abolished. There will still be small, local, humane, sustainable meat producers that will provide meat for special occasions.

In the OBU future, the world will be far better fed and nourished.

In the OBU future, the energy industry will be utterly reconfigured. Fossil fuels will provide only a small portion of energy needs. We will use less energy. Building insulation technologies and regulations will be far, far more effective, so less energy will be wasted. Wind, solar, tide energies will be omnipresent. We will have developed batteries for storing these energies so they can be used most effectively. The oil industry will not have a stranglehold over our politics. When a spokesperson for one of these ancient, arrogant companies speaks, pleading for his ancestral right to rule the planet, the response will usually be laughter.

In the OBU future, the world will have a chance to live, a pretty decent chance.

In the OBU future, the Amazon forests will survive.

In the OBU future, there will be far less worry as to whether there will be a future at all.

In the OBU future, we will still be fighting to save the last glaciers.

The OBU future will not be obsessed with apocalyptic catastrophes. OBU will deflect approaching asteroids with curious space pods and eliminate mass extinctions. There will be almost inconceivably formidable levels of calm. But there will be less boredom. Because there will be far greater degrees of inventiveness, ingenuity, and kindness.

In the OBU future, sea levels will remain constant. For better or worse, Florida will not be lost.

In the OBU future, the opinion of the majority will be a sensible opinion.

In the OBU future, psychic levity and physical levity will combine, and laughter will cause people to float in the air. But gravity will also be valued.

In the OBU future, the unions truly understand that they cannot thrive unless they're fully engaged with the economic, social, political needs of their communities. Unions will be concerned not solely with their members and their contracts. They will be the leaders and focal points of broader working class, anti-plutocratic culture and struggle.

Oligarchy Busters United OBU is

In the OBU future, unions will have good songs again. Everyone will know them and sing them. There will be kick-ass musicians at all union events, but the main songs will be memorable and easy to sing. The music of the movement, sung by all, will blast through all barriers of oppression, ignorance, prejudice, and the privileges and powers of wealth.

But, in the OBU future, unions will be respected, powerful organizations. Most people will belong to one labor union or other, whether or not they work. The unions will be important agents of social cohesion and political power for working people. They will be agents of economic and political power, and also of enjoyment and education. They will have concerts, plays, lectures, films, sports teams.

In the OBU future, education will be valued for real—not just as some statistical aggregate, some set of norms that students at each level should approximate, not as an excuse for kicking the can of poverty and social malfunction down the road a bit further and a bit further, not as some euphemistic consumer "choice" that serves to divide the already divided and to devalue and defund the public schools, not as a pre-vocational or pre-carceral sorting hat that separates the disciplined from the undisciplined.

In the OBU future, teachers at all levels will be known and respected as the wisest, kindest, smartest, most knowledgeable, and most generally valued members of the society. They will not be patronized or condescended to ("Oh, you're teaching children! Well, isn't that wonderful!" –OBU says, give me a fucking break to that!). In the OBU future, teachers will have the same professional status as doctors and lawyers and will be paid comparable wages. Nobody says, "Oh, you decided to become a doctor, you decided to become a lawyer, well isn't that nice! Oh, you decided to become an economist and work at an investment bank, isn't that sweet, that must be so fulfilling!"

Poets will rank not far behind teachers, and be as respected as novelists and architects.

In the OBU future, prosperity will be shared. The most valuable goods, activities, pleasures, relationships will be available to everyone. The rich will not simply take their cut off the top and leave the rest to be fought over, or done without.

In the OBU future, the foregone conclusion will be foregone.

In the OBU future, everyone will participate in making the decisions that affect their lives.

OBU Interlude #4

OBU IS WALKING IN CERTAIN PASTURES AMONG CERTAIN BEASTS.

The beasts are gentle, the beasts are predatory. The beasts have horns, the beasts have very soft but unharvestable fur. OBU is in great danger as it walks without concern through certain pastures.

The pastures are uncertain. They might actually be cities. Growing in the pasture are unseasonably tall trees. The pastures are unconscionably dense in certain places. They are dense with underground burrowing creatures. The gentle predatory beasts love to walk through forests.

OBU loves to walk through public spaces. OBU encounters fellow creatures, with whom public spaces are dense. There is density.

OBU is strangely friendly. OBU wears a smile that has a certain quality of slight uncanniness. There is a disjointedness that is not immediately apparent. OBU finds it difficult to remove its smile, to remove its strangeness, to adjust its certain quality.

And yet a layer of snow makes the city seem a pasture.

All of its eyes contain birds, gray birds. All the gray birds reject the promises that are offered to them. All of the promises lay in the snow. One of them seeks a small brown bird whose home is in the eave of a blue house.

This is one of OBU's residences. But this is an accident.

OBU promises that it will walk across the pasture; it will try to walk across the pasture. OBU promises that it will try to anticipate the underground burrows, the unexpected trees, the sudden flow of the city, the hankering for cold and for blankets when everyone lives on his or her own. There can never be enough blankets or enough unexplained tire marks that end at the edge of a sinkhole that was prematurely repaired.

There is a kingdom of voles, a very harmonious kingdom. The king is Enlightened. He has very little contact with the outside world. Pigeons are his eyes and bats are his ears.

OBU Manifesto #29

Everything that OBU says is obvious.

That greater true democracy should be sought, and tyranny resisted, oppression resisted. That true democracy is not just a political condition but extends to economic and cultural life. That democracy means that people have greater power to determine the material and social and intellectual and spiritual conditions of their lives.

OBU does not apologize for stating the obvious. The obvious is where we begin. How can we move to what may not be obvious until we have reached some agreement as to what is?

Of course, if it's necessary to "reach some agreement," perhaps it is not so obvious after all. We will need to step back a step or two.

OBU is One Big Union. Is this a premise or a conclusion?

OBU observes that 20 people in the United States possess more wealth than the bottom 61% of the population. That piece of data appeared in *The Nation*. OBU hopes that we are not going too far out on a limb to assert that this fact is excessive and obscene.

There is nothing so unique about OBU's opinions and pronouncements. All that is unique about OBU is that it does not exist. For everything else, it seems, exists. Republicans exist; Communists exist; jihadists exist; homeless people exist; Democrats exist; corporate CEOs exist; baseball players exist; heartbreaking works of staggering genius exist; Donald Trump exists; all the characters in all the fictional works ever written exist; the gross national product exists; Apple exists; China exists; Ceylon exists, or does it?; fruits of all kinds exist; animals exist; Fernando Pessoa and Alberto Caeiro exist; all the matter of the earth in aggregate exists, in all its combinations, we need not itemize it further; poverty exists and wealth exists; financial instruments exist; innovative cocktails and overly complicated menus exist; labor unions exist, though not so much; various movements for social justice exist; the great changes to the earth's climate and terrain are coming into existence; history in its textual, material, and psychic forms exists; love and friendship exist; sex exists. Conjugation exists.

Existence is everywhere, one can't avoid it. One can try to find a place of at least relative nullity, but it's no soap, you'll run into for sure whatever you're trying to avoid.

But did we mention the Future? The future is iffy. We launch ourselves toward it like Orville Wright leaping off the dune in his flying winged motorbike, but it doesn't appear that we get there. We glide; or perhaps we crash. Did we mention Death? Death surely is stationed in the "exists" column. Knowledge of death certainly is a legitimate knowledge, even though the knower has not died. After all, most of our knowledge is second-hand, observed or learned, not experienced.

And knowledge, after all, exists. Perhaps knowledge is our meta-category for all other existences.

And this too is obvious, OBU admits. All this is to say that here we are, amid the world of things, people, relationships, mental states, institutions, and all the rest of it. Happiness and sorrow; justice and injustice. Arrogance and humility. And all the rest of it. The world. As such. Such that it cannot contain itself but must always spill over into what we say and keep saying about it.

And in this awful, marvelous plane of existing things, can it be that only OBU does not exist? Must OBU be the Cordelia of this play? Why should a dog, a horse, a rat have life and OBU no breath at all? And she the principle of stringent love: I love you according to my bond, neither more nor less. Then, shortly after, we hear, Nothing comes from nothing. Speak again lest you may mar your fortunes.

Does OBU speak of some "bond"? Which means what? Some set of mutual obligations that people have to each other? Parents to children, for instance, and children to parents. Spouses to each other. Neighbors. Members of religious communities. But these bonds need not be so astringent. The obligation is the debt–but for a loan that never was made.

The obligation may be paid in love, or in dance, or in care, or in work, or in the deep exchange of knowledge through shared actions. Always there is the bond, the powerful transaction of lives lived on the same world.

The world, OBU observes, is deeply in arrears, and yet the wealth exists to pay the debt.

OBU is Oligarchy Busters United

OBU would be the realization. It enjoys a strangely contractual quality. Someone will find it, at the bottom of a drawer or a box. When the light touches it, its dusty particles will leap together and adhere.

OBU Manifesto #30

OBU CALLS FOR A NEW ERA OF HUMILITY. IT IS CLEAR THAT THE LEFT DID NOT RECOGNIZE Trump's appeal and power. The Left did not recognize the damage inflicted on white working class life over the past two generations. It saw but did not acknowledge or work to reverse the destruction of labor unions. It failed to imagine forms of solidarity that would bring together the working class of different races. It lamented, but failed to oppose in significant ways the splitting off of the white working class away from unions, away from the Democratic Party. It failed to imagine inter-racial solidarity.

OBU remarks that the Left was apparently sanguine about the racial barriers, both long-standing and newly invigorated, within the working classes. Yahoos would be Yahoos, appeared to be the attitude, and nothing could be done about it. But luckily, the Left believed, the inexorable demographic trends toward a less white nation would soon get us out of the woods. We let them go, figuring them as merely incorrigible racist, fundamentalist, know-nothing, jackass dimwits. And now they kicked us in the butt and gave us Trump... having previously given us Bush II and Reagan. OBU asks, how had we not gotten that message?

OBU calls for a new era of humility. The Left claims to be the side of solidarity. And yet, solidarity is exactly the zone in which we failed. The Left succeeded in fostering particularities–of gender and race, particularly; and of particular issues like the environment–and derived a theory of "intersectionality" that would bring the particulars together as aggregate political forces. But intersectionality is not solidarity.

OBU is One Big Union. Really.

OBU is not suggesting that emphases on racial, gender, and environmental justice should be left behind or postponed, or that we should now cater or pander to the white conservative voters who despise us. No, that is not the suggestion. But OBU is suggesting humility regarding how much we really know what we're doing. OBU insists that the *goal* of solidarity be foremost in every plan, strategy, and tactic of resistance we devise. It's never just about.... whatever particular issue it's about; it's always also about acting with others, for others, which is acting as/with/for ourselves.

OBU is suggesting always and with tentative insistence and dreadful awareness of its difficulty, the creating of dialogue and of the sites and occasions for dialogue with those outside our general Left-liberal view of the world. OBU recommends humility and openness in these conversations; openness, that is, and respect for the humanity and vulnerability and intelligence of the other. Otherwise, this is not a conversation. There are undoubtedly things we can learn.

But, OBU insists also, there are things they can learn as well, that we will teach. As the confusions, betrayals, incompetencies of the Trump regime become more apparent, it should be clear that this is a moment of humility for the Right. Our commitment, openness, lack of self-righteousness, our humility, the genuineness of our concern, our patience will, OBU hopes, make some impression on their aggressiveness and defensiveness.

We would do well to bring together our responses, views, and analyses of the relatively small group of wealthy, powerful people who largely determine national policy and the allotment of goods. Who are the beneficiaries of the oligarchy's rule? What are the real issues and concerns, and what are the false, merely divisive issues? What consensus, however minimal, might be achieved?

OBU is Oligarchy Busters United

Are such conversations and such minimal consensuses possible, OBU asks?

If they are possible, then let's arrange more of them, all the time and everywhere.

And if they are not possible, really, if no dialogue is possible with people who voted for Trump... well, what then? Then we must win absolute victory. And how will we manage that?

Do we kill them? That seems simultaneously misaligned with our tactical sense, contrary to our moral compass, and, in any event, beyond our skill set, OBU remarks.

The Left, in this country, has never been good at violence. Other places, sure, but not here.

So, what do we do?

We remain

    Determined

        To keep talking (and listening, even though it seems like garbage; who knows when a small change may be detected?)

We continue

            To create

                    Solidarity

                            And work with it

in the new era of humility.

OBU Manifesto #31

OBU SAYS, SO WHAT IF A BUNCH OF PEOPLE FROM DIFFERENT UNIONS AND PEOPLE from different social justice organizations assembled in the same room and talked about how they could work together to empower working people, fight the dictatorship and the war against workers and labor unions, make racial equality a reality, counter global warming, defend threatened minorities and immigrants, and create a better democracy and a just and sustainable economy?

Let's say, the union people were from health care unions, industrial/manufacturing unions, teachers' unions, hotel and restaurant workers' unions, farm workers, the building trades. And let's say the social justice people were from immigrants' rights groups, environmental justice groups, Black Lives Matter groups, prison reform groups, religious denominations, voting rights groups.

Let's call this assemblage, "Labor, Community, Survival, and Power in the Age of Trump." It would address the existential threat to organized labor posed by state and proposed national "right to work" laws, the realization that a coherent progressive political movement needs the organizing expertise and the money of organized labor, the need for unions to look beyond their customary methods of organizing and bargaining–that their mission now cannot be solely for their members, but for all working people; the need to turn the ideological tide away from self-destructive "individualism" that benefits only those already with plenty of resources and toward a new conception of solidarity in which we really are all in this together. This conversation would be a prototype of that solidarity.

OBU wonders, is this a fantasy? Could it really happen? Could even different unions sit at a table and converse constructively? SEIU and UNITE-HERE and Teachers and Teamsters and UAW and Electricians and

Carpenters... OBU will save a place for the Mine Workers.

For what we're facing, nothing we now have is adequate.

For what we're facing, nothing that we've imagined is adequate.

And OBU wonders, could there be, actually, could there come to pass:
ONE BIG UNION???

Why not? OBU will bring them together and lock the door and bring them food and coffee, and they will work it out, figure it out, hammer it through, elevate it, chew on it, originate it, derive the alchemy and the algorithm, yell at each other a lot and call each other idiots and ignorant fools, possibly generate some destructive racially charged commentaries, remember why they're there and what they're facing, and what will happen if they do not succeed. And they will figure it out.

They will figure out and create who they really are.

Why should the hotel workers work with the teachers? And why should the hospital workers work with the electricians? They will understand solidarity in a new way. Who teaches all their children? Who cares for all the sick? Who builds the schools and hospitals and homes and workplaces? Who prepares food? Who grows food? Who makes the city government and town government and state government function? Whose lives do not depend on the work of others? Who is underpaid and unrespected? Who works too many hours? Who works not enough hours? And who profits from the hours worked and not worked?

How can these different unions work together? OBU asks, how can they not work together?

Unless there is OBU, there will be nothing. The Labor "Movement" cannot be a movement unless it is OBU.

And why should immigrant rights groups or racial justice groups or the ACLU or environmental justice groups or food justice groups or LBGTQ groups or the whole array of progressive causes work with any of these unions or, indeed, work with each other? Because the unions still have resources in people, skills, and money that no one else on the Left can muster. Union rank and file may not be on the cutting edges of progressive terminologies–but they too are being systematically exploited and attacked. The struggle has many avenues, but it's one struggle.

OBU is Oligarchy Busters United

OBU is One Big Union

OBU often hears people say, why should union members get the privilege of decent health insurance, some kind of pension, better wages? Why should they get that and the rest of us don't? Why should they have some special status? (As if it were that easy).

And OBU hears union members respond, well, turn that around... Why don't *you guys* organize, form a union and get yourself some better wages and benefits. (As if it were that easy).

But OBU contend that both are wrong! They're wrong insofar as they're right. They're right insofar as they're wrong. The point is to get a decent, respected status for *all* work. Unions must expand their concept of whom they represent. Unions are threatened with extinction, and *for that reason* must think of their mission more broadly. Unions now must understand themselves as working for all workers. They must organize and expand as well as they're able, but must always keep the non-unionized workers in their strategies. And non-unionized workers in the age of "Right to Work" laws must come, however slowly and painfully, to understand that what money they save in not paying union dues will be extracted mercilessly in every other transaction of their economic lives.

New forms of solidarity must be imagined and brought into being.

OBU is the embarking and the arriving.

OBU is always cutting to the chase. But OBU knows that it's a long pursuit.

OBU Manifesto #32

OBU ASKS, IF THERE HAD BEEN CLASS SOLIDARITY ON THE TITANIC, COULD THE SHIP have been saved?

Of course not. But the analogy is unsuitable, as is every analogy that places a singular event in the role of a social world and global economy.

How many times, OBU asks wearily, do we see a guy pull out some anecdote or some hypothetical or some hypothetical anecdote or anecdotal hypothetical, and then say, there, see? I told you! And then he looks so pleased and smug as if he'd just belched out all the proofs from Euclid, Leibniz, Poincare, and Grigori Perelman, plus the entire lived experience of the human species, placed in on a small platter, named it Exhibit A—and concluded, well, you know, this just stands for all of that, so what have *you* got?

And OBU says, I've got nothin', same as yesterday. If the ship goes down, we go down with it. That's solidarity. If the orchestra goes down, we all go down.

OBU asks, Where the hell are *you* going?

OBU says, there's nothing wrong with good technology. More on that later.

OBU will ban the synecdoche. There is no part that stands for the whole— or that stands for it with any real accuracy. The synecdoche proves nothing. No metaphor proves anything. On the other hand, no argument really *proves* anything. And it's becoming disturbingly evident that even no *evidence* apparently proves anything—to anyone not already disposed to believe it.

The only salient demonstration of truth at this point is satire and parody.

Take what is, and what is already absurd and horrific, and make the absurdity gigantic, like a Thanksgiving parade balloon, and let the balloons of our political world bounce against each other saying exactly what they say in their human forms, and then laugh as if each peal and bellow were your last; laugh as if the world was ending. And avoid the subjunctive. "As if..."

Well. OBU admits. That brings us back to metaphor. OK, we'll let it back in. But it still proves nothing.

OBU IS ONE BIG UNION

Satire and parody have been the only orders of truth, OBU asserts, since the election of 2000, and its concussive echo of September 2001. OBU is not alleging causality. Just: there was the one shock, and then the next. And which was the greater shock, in retrospect? The security lapse, act of terror, loss of life, rush into needless war, implementation of new security state... or violent gouging out of essential organs of democracy? Tough call. The fact of the first set the stage for the consequences of the second. An illegitimate government is prone to poor judgements, to recklessness. No matter how macho and blustery its language and actions, it's always looking around the room for an escape route, like a gangster in a crowded restaurant.

The fall of the Towers, then, was the fall of our Tower of Babel–the end of what was left of any common language. That's when the national facades of civility and decency were knocked off–they were already just facades, of course. It was Karl Rove who said that the Democratic Party (and let's just say, the Left in general, in the broadest sense) was doomed because it still inhabited a reality-based world. The new politics consisted of creating its own reality, which its opponents would then have to react to.

So, is solidarity across or even within social class, across or even within race, across or even within gender, geographical region, nation, profession or vocation–are all these ideas of solidarity romantic illusions, or some sort of illusion?

OBU asks, what is the distinction between an illusion and an aspiration?

Can we say that all that now *illudes* us was once only aspired to?

Is the idea of solidarity a kind of bridge across the chasm of separated, competing individuals speaking untranslatable languages–a bridge that we can build only once we've crossed it?

OBU is under the distinct impression that people from different groups, locales, cultures, races, economic strata, educational levels really do not know each other. They have neither deep experience, acquired familiarity, nor learned information. What they appear to have in mind are distorted, insulting caricatures. Those self-righteous, pretentious pc assholes; those ignorant rube racist morons. And of course those niggers–no adjectives necessary.

OBU does not know whether knowledge, experience, and empathy can convert years of sediments of resentment, self-righteousness, ignorance, and meanness of spirit into a field ready to support solidarity.

Ah! So, OBU is a religion now? It seeks conversion?

OBU is not a religion.

OBU is Oligarchy Busters United!

OBU Manifesto #33

Religions provide sets of obligations. They are called laws, but they are better understood as obligations. You are obligated to do them, whether or not there are means of enforcement or worldly consequences for not doing them. There are not necessarily reasons for doing them, though reasons can always be invented. Their foundation, theologically, is God (there's a tautology!), but the obligation is independent of its origin. One feels the obligation because the obligation is an obligation (that's actually *not* a tautology!). One *can* do otherwise, but one *ought* not. Really, one has no choice.

Muley Graves in Steinbeck's *The Grapes of Wrath*: he is cooking a rabbit. Tom Joad and the Preacher approach him. "You gonna share that rabbit, Muley?" asks the Preacher. "Well, I reckon I ain't got no choice," says Muley. "I don't mean that like it sounds," he continues. "It's just, if a fellow is hungry and another fellow has some food, well then, that fellow ain't got no choice but to give part of it to the hungry fellow." That's the nature of obligation.

Enlightenment political philosophy provided discourses of rights. Rights are specific freedoms or entitlements possessed by every person. There are freedoms *to* perform some social or private action; and there are freedoms *from* some external power abrogating one's actions, political status, or property. The right to free speech and assembly; to think freely; the right to not be searched without cause; the right to equal protection by the law; or, freedom from fear and want;

or, the right to health care or the right to employment. Rights can be contested. New rights can be formulated.

Obligations, being moral in character, seem to be self-evident, self-justifying. Rights, being political, are generally given divine or natural foundations. "We are endowed by our Creator," etc. the enunciators of rights wish them to be self-evident, but they are not. Why? Because they must be struggled for. Their foundations are shaky and fictional. God? Nature? Sure, tell me another one.

Rights have their origins in exercises of power. Once established in constitutions or customs, they become conventional, and one may believe if one likes that their origins rest in God or Nature, or in the fiction of the social contract. And yet, it is important that people believe that these rights inhere in them. If people believe they possess these rights *inalienably*, then they will fight to preserve them. In Mozart's early (brilliant, gorgeous, hilarious, highly orientalist, and Enlightenment) opera, *The Escape from the Seraglio* (1782), the Sultan's brutish (though comically ineffectual) servant attempts to sexually molest the British heroine's maidservant. In rejecting his advances, she tells him, "I am an English woman, born to freedom!" (*Ich bin eine Englanderin, zur Freiheit geboren*). And yet she is not free. Or, she is and is not. She is free internally; externally, she is in bondage. Fortunately, since the drama is a comedy, she triumphs; she and her mistress escape with their respective true loves. Or rather, the Sultan, whom Mozart renders as the only truly rational character in all of opera—he is so rational, in fact, that he does not sing!—releases them. Why does he release them? Because they have rights? Surely not. He has power over them. Whatever rights they have, they cannot exercise. He releases them because

he is *obligated* to release them.

But just as those with rights are often powerless to exercise them, those with power are often unwilling to act on their obligations. Thus, the powerless are obligated, and the powerful are free. This tipsy contrivance of rights, power, and duty plays out clearly in contemporary politics. The poor are enjoined to all sorts of moral obligation in order to receive their stipends from the moralizing welfare apparatus. The wealthy feel no obligations at all. If they give to charity, they give *freely*. Their giving is part of their freedom.

One does not fight in order to experience obligation. One fights for one's rights, for one's freedoms. But even if one wins, or especially if one wins, obligation remains. Obligation is tied to us. It cannot be shaken off or severed.

To refuse the obligation is to be damned. Cursed. Stripped of one's costume. The Emperor is naked not simply because of a childish vanity and love of extravagance which is exploited by the clever pseudo-tailors. He is naked because he rejects the obligations that give all of us our social garments and currencies. Our obligations, our moral positioning in the world, are what clothe us, and if we shed them, all our garments are illusions. As with the Emperor, the illusion is only enforced by power.

OBU Manifesto #34

OBU OBSERVES, OR OPINES, THAT THE "MODERN AGE" CAN BE CHARACTERIZED BY sets of conceptual revolutions, guised as revelations, or as "discoveries." We can list them: Copernican, Newtonian, Locke/Rousseauian, Industrial, Darwinian, Marxian, Freudian, capitalist-technological especially in its global aspect, revolutionary reversals in understandings of gender and of race which cannot be written in the shorthand of single names– and corresponding revolutions/revelations in art and philosophy, and scholarship in various fields.

OBU adds that all of these have a certain apocalyptic sensibility: the old age is gone, utterly wiped clean; a new form of understanding, of being, has replaced it. We used to think "X", but now we know "Not-X." The breaks are sudden, violent, disorienting. Or they are sudden, then slowly disseminate, then exert, both quickly and slowly, their gigantic techtonic impacts and diremptions.

The changes and ruptures are fundamental. For what is shifted? The very notion of the human relation to the universe: the place of the earth in the cosmos, the place of the human in the biological order, the relation of a person to his own self, social relations of class, authority, legitimacy, one's identity as a gendered being, the human relation to some supernatural, all-powerful, creative, moral, nurturing and punishing force... "All that is solid melts into air," as we used to say.

And this process, OBU reflects, is called, in various inflections, "progress." Its caricature and undoing we see in Walter Benjamin's famous "angel of history."The angel, blown forward toward the future but looking backward, sees only undifferentiated heaps of ruin–"and that we call 'progress.'" Sure, undoubtedly.

Yet each time we rebuild from these ruins, each time more sumptuously, we (or those of us of certain social/intellectual categories) celebrate again at least *our own* versions of this story of apocalyptic progress–the story of conceptual revelation through science and rigorous thought and creativity. We critique the wrong, oppressive, wasteful, destructive paths toward which our apocalyptic progress has swerved, but on the whole the Revolution/Revelation of European Enlightenment remains our central article of faith.

Even the so-called "posthuman" is another iteration of an already de-centered humanism, now incorporated with new technologies, animals, objects, flattened subjectivities, etc. But it requires an unflattened subject to imagine the flattening. No, that brief human imprint in the sand that Foucault apocalyptically invoked is still trudging along the beach looking for a hotel bar where it might get a drink. It's a thirsty trudge, that's for sure.

OBU is certainly thirsty. Its human subjectivities are ready to put down a couple of cold ones.

But, while we are thinking and drinking, and feeling pretty good, after all, that the final revelation has been received, this view is not universal.

OBU is One Big Union

OBU tends to ridicule the "end of history"/"end of ideology" theories– the Daniel Bell, Francis Fukuyama crowd. It's silly. History continues. Ideological conflict continues. Nothing is over, for God's sake, nothing is over till we end the world definitively.

And yet, OBU is trying to be honest, do we not feel that the fundamental decenterings and demystifications and secularization and transformations of divine authority into more-or-less social contract theories of justice and something-resembling-democratic-governance with guarantees of minority rights and basic equality, and the movement of divine spirit into aesthetic production and of soul into psyche, and the determination to expand the initially limited range of justice (which permitted imperialism, constructions of race, continued suppression of women, industries of extraction and destruction... and other depravities) to include everyone... that all these notions are now set and settled; that these revelations are the real deal, if only we would receive them truly and act on them!

Isn't that correct? Enlightenment is *Enlightenment*. We critique Enlightenment–the constant vocation we are called to–but critique is an essential part of Enlightenment. The doctrine of Enlightenment is that we require more of it, and we are *obligated* to seek it. Enlightenment does not come down from the Mountain. "It is not in heaven" (Deut. 30.12), but emerges from open human dialogue and thinking.

And we believe this emphatically. This is true. Truth is the ultimate destination of human dialogue.

OBU is Oligarchy Busters United

OBU believes dogmatically in anti-dogmatism.

(Anti-)OBU Manifesto (#35)

The spirit of OBU is as mean-spirited as everyone else. You think it's not?

Why should anyone think they're any better than anyone else?

OBU sees through your bullshit, for starters. OBU is looking over your shoulder right now, reading your repulsive thoughts that you think no one can see.

OBU knows exactly how stupid you are.

Get with the program. There isn't any "Big Union." It's complete bullshit. Who the hell would be in it anyway?

The spirit of OBU is filled with boundless contempt. OBU plans to have a drink and plop down and see what's on TV. OK, the Knicks are playing Milwaukee, that should be enought to trigger a major depressive episode. God forbid OBU's remote might set upon MSNBC and maybe see Rachel or, more horrifically, Chris Matthews, or, more suicidally, Brian Williams. Better to watch the Knicks stink out the joint and imagine them all with Trump hairdos.

OK, OBU says, basically, go fuck yourself.

OBU says, you vapid bullshit liberals who think you can find some middle way and have no idea how the power of capital operates: Fuck you.

And OBU says, you self-righteous Leftist ineffectual dipsticks with your constant haranguing anyone who uses the wrong language: you can absolutely and without equivocation go fuck yourselves.

And OBU doesn't want to hear about your queer bullshit and your trans bullshit and what personal pronoun you prefer. Fuck you and go fuck yourselves.

And OBU is tired of the fucking Jews and their self-righteous, moralizing crap. They were so down with the civil rights movement back in the day that now they think they can just enjoy their prosperity and scream about anti-semitism on college campuses and Israel boycotts. Fuck Israel. Fuck the Jews.

And while we're on the subject, OBU says, fuck the BDS people too and their hypocritical crypto-anti-semitism.

Also, fuck Palestine. Fuck two-states, fuck one-state, and fuck every conceivable configuration of states in the Middle East.

And fuck you, Black Lives Matter. OBU doesn't like to see black people get killed by police. But–hate to be a buzz-kill–but there really is a lot of violence in a lot of black neighborhoods, and it's not all coming from police. So, fuck your self-righteous, posturing, gestural politics that ignores the economics of race and class and burns every possible bridge that doesn't circle back to its own righteous victimhood.

And while we're on the subject: Fuck the police. Really.

And OBU now is almost too exhausted to say... Fuck you, Trump. Yeah. What else is new. But, once more with feeling. Yes. Trump, just take a moment from your duties and pleasures of office, and stick something enormous and gnarly up your ass, and then send us all a good tweet, would ya? And fuck all your staff and fuck all your cabinet appointments. Fuck the Republican congress and senate. And all you good folks who voted for Trump, fuck you in spades. When there's no safe air, water, food; no working transportation system; no functioning schools; no public space that hasn't been wrecked, gutted, profited from and abandoned; when a new war starts that we have not a clue how to wage, win, get out of–or probably even locate; when, when you're sick, you just go somewhere and die...

To all of you, and to any that OBU has not specified: Fuck you and go fuck yourself.

OBU IS NOTHING. OBU IS SHIT.

OBU Interlude #4

Why can't we be nihilists?

Why can we only be nihilists?

Why can we not be poets?

Why can we only be poets?

Because the air is not yet poisoned?

Because children are born and the burden of shared mortality is too great.

Because we see the mother cat licking her stillborn kitten for hours before she gives up, even as she nurses the two live ones.

Because our lives are lived in symbols, and mourning is both symbolic and not symbolic.

Because our sexual drives and desires wear symbolic fabric; even our nakedness is a representation.

Because one puts on and puts off; because we eat-digest-excrete; because we breathe; because at a certain point, we know we are withering; because we forestall... we exercise, we try to eat better, we become more cautious drivers, we play musical instruments or games of skill to keep our synapses lubricated and exercised.

Because it is in the absolute nature of experience to be in debt. It is essential to our being to be insufficient.

Because we are born helpless, and people must take care of us to help us grow into maturity.

Our symbolic fenestration is always cracked. It is our comic destiny to be always humiliated.

Because we are temporary.

The filing cabinet of nothing can hold everything you put in it and it will still be empty, and you can live there, and live in truth.

But there are other cabinets.

OBU Manifesto #36

No action is wasted, OBU asserts. Every act of solidarity has value and meaning. OBU repeats, do not give up and do not lose energy, determination, and hope. Did we think this was a short struggle, after all these small and large advances and after all the long stumbles and defeats?

OBU recognizes that the election of Trump is not only dangerous in many ways and likely to increase the ratios of injustice, inequality, ignorance, and violence. His election was also humiliating. How could the president of our country—elected legally, though dubiously—be *this guy*, one of the greatest hucksters, cheaters, and buffoons this nation has ever produced?! And how can we continue to tolerate, much less venerate, an electoral system that can put in office someone who received three million votes less than his opponent? What could we possibly call such a system? So, both these facts—the man elected and the method by which he was elected—are causes for deep humiliation.

The humiliation, OBU urges, we can and must get past. OBU is the power that will reimagine democracy.

OBU is Oligarchy Busters United

Be in persistent communication with legislators. Be part of demonstrations.

But moreover and more than this, OBU implores, locate and cleave to the social and political soulmates of your lives. Those friends you have, and their adoption tried, grapple them to your soul with hoops of steel. And move beyond them. OBU urges that this be the Great Moment and Age of the Potluck! OBU says, bring people together—old friends and new friends, new acquaintances, people you'd like to have as friends, old cronies and people of different classes, races, religions... and even some people with different political views. Let all be invited and none be turned away!

No action is wasted. Every act of solidarity exerts power.

OBU is One Big Union

OBU acknowledges and experiences humiliation, despair, and rage.

OBU is looking up from the ground right now, or looking up from some pit that it's fallen into. Every few days it finds itself down there again, and thinks, Oh shit, how the fuck do I pull myself out of this? And OBU responds, well, psychically, individually, it's not so hard to hoist oneself upright again... Being with kids and other loved ones helps; playing music helps; immersing oneself in whatever has meaning and joy generally works. And those things still exist in abundance... We haven't reached the true dystopic hell-zone just yet. It's still possible to get up, laugh, and get moving.

And that's a good thing because pulling ourselves out from the collective ditch is not nearly so easy. The possibility of individual happiness and hope is crucial to the larger struggle, OBU contends. We can't prevail and achieve justice and democracy if all of us are trapped in our emotional abysses.

OBU is the movement out of the abyss.

OBU is the movement that identifies and contests unjust congealments of power, that contests the disproportionate power of wealth, that addresses the extraordinary power of ignorance and fear.

OBU is the relaxation of muscles we don't need, and the activation of the muscles we do.

OBU Manifesto #37

OBU BELIEVES DOGMATICALLY IN ANTI-DOGMATISM.

OBU does not see this as a problem, but there it is. Yet, what if, say, some divine, omniscient, etc. entity made itself known to us directly and said, yeah, those traditional religion cats have been right all along and I was just messing with you for all these millennia, making you think I wasn't for real... well, OBU supposes that would be a different kettle of fish.

And then we cancelled and chagrined Enlightened ones would have a few options: We could say, OK God, we see your light, we are your servants in love, etc. Or we could go Luciferian (the darker light) and actively rebel. Or we could go Talmudic and say that supernatural revelation determines nothing and we'll continue our human dialogue in search of human truth— and hope that God has a sense of humor about that. And there's also the Ivan Karamazov/Grand Inquisitor response, in case God turns out to be Christian and incarnate.

But OBU is pretty sure, is really quite decided, that this speculation is strictly hypothetical; that we're on our own figuring it out, and that is the final Revelation.

So: Enlightenment is not some other "God that Failed." It is the not-god that we shall follow and fail on our own. And our failures thus far are clear and well-documented–in the broadest terms, the insertion of false Universals as occasions for the suppression and exploitation of people outside the ruling cliques, the general construction and stigmatization of "others."

"Justice, Justice shall you pursue." Fair enough?

But, OBU is aware–speaking of history not having ended–that the old Traditional, Old Time Religion population, even after having been thoroughly debunked, discredited, kicked in the keister, forced to take its medicine, dragged into modernity, patiently lectured, lovingly reeducated, exasperatingly endured, *somehow* has not expired and has not been convinced or converted.

They are still here, living in the elder-alt-world of the young earth, inserted fossils, and deceptive geostrata, the coming of the End-Times, the nearness of the Lord/Father/Son and His Salvation, the eternal truths of Man and Woman, the constant reality of Sin, the fallibility of science, the certainty of prophecy, the secular bias of media, the poisonous propaganda of public education. These are the Christian checkpoints, most visible and powerful in the U.S., but there are Jewish and Muslim equivalents.

And these traditional, archaic—to us, vestigial; to us, sheerly ignorant— outlooks are not unintelligent; are both consistent and, tactically, quite clever. The pre-modern traditionalists have learned to use, and use with a certain apparent glee, the tools of Enlightenment in the service of turning it back. They use the idea of "relativism," for instance. If, they say, one rejects some ultimate *foundation* of thought, action, ethics, history, etc. well, then, isn't everything then possible and permissible– any fact, any version of science, any political tactic? If the revelations at Sinai and Golgotha are denied, and the various revelations of decentering are accepted in their place, and then there is no center, well, then, there is no truth... (Of course, they contend, they know what the truth is really– it is what it always was; the new revelations are lies and deceptions). And so, then, *everything is relative; everything is positional.* Evolution is just a "theory," or an opinion. Every opinion is as good as another. The new post-Enlightenment scientific-philosophical-administrative junta has no legitimacy. The Enlightenment dupes claim the legitimacy of evidence and logic? Fine, we'll produce "evidence" and "logic." How is ours inferior to theirs? Climate change is a hoax. Look, here's the evidence and theory. Their journals use "peer review," and thus unveil that process as empty... There's always *somebody*, or a group of somebodies, who will say *anything.*

So, how do we know anything? Except in God?

So, there we are, circa 1300 or so.

This circumstance, for OBU, is, obviously, not acceptable.

The pre-modern Traditionalists work under the auspices of complete misunderstanding, obviously. But how is one to convince them of this, given that they reject our quaint and heretical notion of "fact"? Everyone has opinions and, if you believe Heisenberg–and every fundamentalist must have his paraphrase of Heisenberg—facts are mutable too. Everything's embedded in some narrative, in the point of view of some observer; nothing in this earthly, secular realm is reliable. The anti-Enlightenment wants to return to the stability of the pre-Enlightenment theocentric universe. There are indeed *facts*; but when the theocrats play on the secular pitch, they feel privileged not to use them because they believe the secularists themselves have abandoned truth, so all's fair.

OBU is forced to surmise that this conflict is a religious war; and if this is true, then it can only end badly. And so, we must not let it end. OBU believes we might well abandon our apocalyptic/progressive view of history, in which Enlightened Modernity (including all its amendments, past and future) is the last revelation/dispensation. Progress is just our idea of being right. The future may well be a new medievalism. The character of the future will be the result of struggle.

OBU is committed to ensuring that this struggle is verbal. OBU is committed to winning this struggle–but on terms that nearly everyone will be willing to accept.

OBU IS OLIGARCHY BUSTERS UNITED

OBU will conceive spaces where conversations can take place. The more the better; preferably everywhere, in the Red Zones and the BUBs. OBU will search for points of agreement–places where a "pro-life" position, for instance, will have to coincide with needs for greater social justice, greater resources allotted to health care, education, leisure and other components of a good and flourishing *life*. OBU will stress the practical benefits of science for life. OBU will be happy to engage in the sharing of Biblical texts, and will stress the abundance of modes of interpreting these texts... I'll read it your way if you read it my way, and her way, and a few other ways.

Can we do this, OBU asks, or would we prefer to kill each other?

And what, OBU wonders, might we concede in these conversations? We will be asking a lot of the Traditionalist crowd–asking them, above all perhaps, to allow (at least for the purposes of conversation) for a certain pluralness where they would prefer a sanctified singleness. And so, what might our One Big Union be willing to concede?

OBU will not concede to threats and exclusions directed against minorities of race, religion, gender, etc. OBU will always present arguments for an expanded idea of a public good; yet would concede, I think, the acceptability of private property and of a market economy (with regulations and obligations to be discussed and negotiated). OBU would support wholeheartedly and in the strongest terms freedom of religion in its clear (we think) First Amendment sense: freedom of belief and practice of religion in the context of a plurality of religions. No one can tell another person what to believe and what, if any, religion to practice. We would all, OBU hopes (and prays?!) agree to this. But the belief and practice of religion must not extend into determining policies in the public sphere. There can be no official or unofficial national religion. OBU loves Christians. Christians are great! Christians are top-notch! Best art and music in the world (or at least it used to be; Bach, Fra Angelico–can't beat 'em). Bravo to the whole operation! But the governing of the country is secular.

The governing of the country is secular. Discussions of the derivation of national laws and constitutions and whether and how they bear relation to religious laws and principles are very interesting. But the governing of the country is secular. And you may pray five times a day, go to Bible study three nights a week, wear a kippah and hijab together at the same time, and say "Merry Christmas" every day of the year, says OBU; but the governing of the country is secular.

OBU Manifesto #38

OBU IS EXASPERATED! OH, SURE, OBU HAS COMFORTINGLY RECITED, WE'LL FIND common ground with the working class Trumpistas; we'll have fruitful dialogues with Christian fundamentalists, featuring deep discussions of who should throw the first stone and why John 8.7 is actually an anti-semitic afterthought since the rabbis of that time were in fact opposed to capital punishment and tried to make it as rare as possible and Jesus' attitude there was actually mainstream and not oppositional. We'll talk it out and eventually it will all be good. No stones thrown.

Right, OBU says, good luck with that.

OBU's feeling sympathy with the exasperated Emerson, that "this conformity makes them not false in a few particulars, authors of a few lies, but false in all particulars. Their every truth is not quite true. Their two is not the real two, their four not the real four: so that every word they say chagrins us and we know not where to begin to set them right."

But maybe that's not OBU's job—to change their language game, to "set them right." OBU's job is to build solidarity first among those already inclined to share it; to imagine this solidarity, make it visible, increase it. Not everyone will want it. But once a critical mass of solidarity has been achieved, well, there it will be; it will be part of the political fabric.

The graphic emblem of OBU is the limit and the passing of the limit, the move from one circle to the concentric space beyond it and to the one beyond that.

Who of us, really, has reached his or her limits? Is there not always a further step? Do we ever really stop developing? Can we look at someone and say, there, that's where this person will stop; she will go no further? He can only repeat himself, there is no more to see or hear, there is no more to know? Would we say this of ourselves?

Or people can give up. Or they give up though they don't know they've given up. They feel they're still searching, but they've lost the sense of how that is done, how the search is to be carried out. The compass has malfunctioned–some electric despair in the brain has pulled it off kilter–and when they think they're going forward, they've only moved sideways. The body's own psycho-propriocentric knowledge is usually accurate, they feel (we feel): the inner sense we have of where we are, who we are, where we're facing, which way is up, which way is forward, which way is home, are our bodies in balance, our limbs in proportion, our frontal lobes and amygdalas well connected, which ways are known and which are unknown. But sometimes we feel unsure and want to trust our *instruments*. An experienced hiker friend once told us, when I'm lost in the woods, if my sense of direction differs from the compass, I trust the compass. But in the case of being lost within, or in the case of the social body and psyche being lost, what instruments or what senses do we trust, with so many senses and instruments pressing against and inside us?

You can't tell who is still confronting their old limits and who is configuring new ones. People may remain productive, succeed at their work, take up new pastimes, demonstrate new commitments, find new lovers, but still be restricted by the old limits, unable to go past them, unable perhaps even to recognize them. Or a person might remain at the same station, in the same relationship, apparently stagnant and hopeless, and yet inside is experiencing explosions from some source in the infinitesimal amplitudes beyond the apparent–new plethoras of image, emotion, conception. The person smiles at you from somewhere else, and you glimpse, or you might glimpse, in that moment a place you've surely never been, and there she is; she's there. You would never have guessed.

OBU is the place between limits. OBU is on the verge of.

OBU are...

OBU IS ONE BIG CONTESTATION AND AFFIRMATION UNITED AND UN-OSSIFIED

OBU Manifesto #39

OBU CONCURS, WITH WALT WHITMAN, "ONLY WHAT PROVES ITSELF TO EVERY MAN and woman is so, Only what nobody denies is so."

And OBU remarks that if that's the case, then not very much is true these days, for not much is agreed on.

And OBU would like to insist on clarity and would like to put obscurity in its proper place. Obscurity is precious, it should be revered, for much that is precious is also obscure. But the beauty and value of obscurity is that the dark and hidden can cut through one as sharply as the brightest light... if one can get the language right.

And OBU repeats, "These are the thoughts of all people in all ages and lands. If they are not yours as much as ours, they are nothing or next to nothing... If they are not just as close as they are distant, they are nothing."

OBU does not believe that disrupting grammar and syntax is a revolutionary act.

But OBU feels stuck now in its terminal. It is waiting for its train, which is its terminology. Only the right terms will take it from the terminal. A term is a vehicle and a goal. A term indicates where its idea will terminate. Without the right terms, OBU fears, its progress will be only intermittent.

The problem of political language and entreaty, OBU reflects, is really a problem of mobility. How do you get from one cognitive/affective place—one place of thought and feeling and experience and reflection–to another place, or the place of another. Our words for how language works are geographical. *Metaphor* means "to carry across," to carry meaning from one context to another, which means to create a new meaning that works somewhat differently in its two (or more) locations. And *metaphor* is the Greek synonym for the Latin *translation*, which means–identically– "to carry across." Every translation is a metaphor, every metaphor a translation. And every missive transmitted to another must, if it is to provide meaning, become something new as it is received. A *transmission* is something "sent across."

What wonderful neural capacities we have to do all this loading and shipping and unloading, and what amazing work it is to *understand* when symbols fly at us like barrages of balls and kites and knives and diving paper airplanes and large ungainly packages we have no idea what they are and tiny slivers of ungraspable substance that get into our eyes and nostrils like mist.

OBU is One Big Union

George Herbert wrote that prayer, the quintessential verbal jettison, was, in the end, "something understood."

OBU might be willing to consider these Manifestos as forms of prayer.

But beyond all this, OBU posits, there is the untranslatable–the place withdrawn and extended outside the meaningful flux of our symbols, the things at the core and in the workings of our bodies, sensations, visceral emotions; and there are the large things, the systemic and global functions and manifestations for which our terminologies lack terminals and translations. We know what we can say about these things, and we know that we're not getting it right. We must resort to *catachresis*– the word for the thing or process for which we don't have a word; thus, necessarily, the wrong word, the word outside the network of words, the word that refuses to be carried across, that stays where it is, and you must come to it. The singular utterance.

OBU is learning to navigate.

Is this what poetry is, OBU wonders. The language that rejects all paraphrase and summary. Poetry can only be translated poorly. To translate it well requires that you transform it. People ask, what does a poem mean? And one can only answer, it means what it says. What you say *about* it is not what it means. It means what it says. Thus, you must read it. In the curved space of the untranslatable, the poem may have been sent to you (as its launch is both private and universal), but you still must go to it. It will not be where you think you saw it, and you cannot judge its location by its trajectory. Missing it one place, seek it another.

Whatever is commonest and cheapest and nearest and easiest is OBU.

OBU is the most obscure and secret, but OBU is tactful; it knows that not every inmost place should be illuminated.

OBU is what we bring to each other, whatever we are willing to bring.

OBU Manifesto #40

BUT THEN THERE'S THE QUESTION OF *ABORTION*. OBU IS GIVEN TO UNDERSTAND that abortion is one really sore and inflexible point of difference between the Enlightened secular OBUists and the traditionalist anti-Enlightenment (mostly) Christian antagonists. There are many people for whom abortion is the single salient issue of electoral politics and general moral-political orientation. OBU is hesitant even to get into it. Either human life existentially-spiritually begins (and legally should begin) at conception, and so to end embryonic or fetal life is murder; or, human life begins at birth, or at some definable point of viability, and so ending the life of embryo or non-viable fetus is not murder, and its existence should be under the authority of the woman carrying the embryo or fetus. Those are heavy stakes in either direction.

Are human beings to have to control over their procreative powers? And, if not–if procreation must have its own, or have divine, agency—are women alone to bear the brunt of that lack of authority? Men are granted control, at least in theory, over their bodies and the products of their labor. To lack control over one's body and its labor is to be a slave. Are women to be deprived of this same control? Are women, in effect, to be slaves of their reproductive capacities? And, one might say, OBU continues, that birth, the exit of the becoming-child from the mother's body, is a sensible moment from which to document the beginning of a human life. We celebrate, after all, a person's birthday. We become legal entities on the occasion of our births, as documented by our birth certificates. One's birth is not a trivial event. It is the beginning of one's life *as a person*.

At the same time, OBU reflects, fetal or embryonic life is, indeed life; and it is, genetically, human life. What else could it be? Whatever its existential or legal status–as not-yet person, not-yet on the census–and putting aside the spiritual question of its possible "ensoulment," this life is certainly regarded as having value. Mothers and fathers-to-be will go to enormous lengths, make great sacrifices and take great risks to protect the life the mother is carrying. This life will be their child–even though it is not yet a child, not yet a legally counted member of the population–and they will do anything to protect it. If it is born prematurely, they will bring to bear every medical assistance to preserve its life. If it is lost, they will grieve for its loss. Fetal life is precious. Its gestation is long. The mother's protective apparatus for the child-in-process is impressively resilient.

OBU IS, TENTATIVELY, ONE BIG UNION

And yet again, as OBU grasps not for the first or the last time, human lives are complicated and difficult. Biological being is often not so well aligned with social, psychological, and moral being. The biological imperative to bear the child conflicts with economic pressures and the needs and desires of individual lives. And OBU recalls that the biological imperative is itself not infrequently truncated by miscarriages and premature deliveries and, in the days before modern medicine, by horrendous numbers of maternal deaths in childbirth. In our evolutionary rush to increase cranial size and to stand upright, it appears our female reproductive physiology did not keep pace. The curse of Eve, it seems, was not disobedience, but intelligence, as brain size exceeded pelvic capacity!

But here we are, OBU regrets to say, still at an impasse. The preceding set of clever reflections will be utterly rejected by the religious opponent of abortion rights. For, of course, what OBU has neglected here is God and God's wishes and commands. Human beings have souls. These souls enter the first cell of the zygote. The biological, corporeal container of the soul, whatever its developmental status, is sacred. All souls and their containers are equal in the eyes of God. Q.E.D.

OBU would not want to be a buzzkill at this point and question how exactly one determines the wishes of God on this and other matters, or ask why such fervent political energy on an issue which elicits so little scriptural attention, and why this fervor is not applied to questions of, say, social justice on which scripture has so much more to say... But no matter, let's take the position as sincere and credible.

Fine, says OBU, let's talk. If the question is one of life over death, then let's talk about it. OBU would like to think that it prefers life to death in the vast majority of instances and, indeed, as a general principle. Then let's try honestly to reach some points of potential consensus on topics where life is at stake. Are you willing to do it? OBU is ready. We have to talk about environmental issues where the life of the planet is at stake. And our hypothetical Christian interlocutor has to give something here. This is not something to mess around with. This is the real deal. It's more important than, say, capital punishment. OBU does not believe the state should take lives, but if there are sufficient safeguards, appeal procedures, DNA testing, and perhaps some "Let he who is without sin" clause in place–if it is certain that the penalty is applied fairly, consistently, and only to the most outrageous crimes, then, OK, that's something we can talk about. So, we'll give you some form of death penalty if you'll acknowledge the need to invest in energy and economic policies that will protect the lived-in world. If it means throwing a few legitimately evil guys under the bus, so be it.

And for abortion, OBU will give you this. OBU opposes abortion. OBU will commit itself to making abortion as infrequent as possible. OBU cannot take the position that abortion should be illegal. OBU will not renounce a woman's legal right to have an abortion. Abortion should be a medical procedure that is legal and available to women who require or desire it. But: Let's work together to make abortion so unnecessary as to be nearly inconceivable–sorry for the pun, didn't notice it till it was already in the sentence. First, let's make contraception inexpensive and accessible. Second, let's improve the accessibility, quality, and affordability of child care. Third, let's make health care truly universal and affordable. And if that means bringing in some Canadian or European or Australian style single payer system, then that's what we have to do. Are you with us? Are you serious about life or is this just a game? Let's make this society truly hospitable to children! Health care, child care, education, recreational facilities, after school arts programs, sports programs available to everyone, psychological counseling services in every school. Let's make a "pro-life" agenda–OBU is down with that big time. OBU cannot share the metaphysical position of the Christian anti-abortion groups, but OBU is happy to be opposed to abortion. We want to work with all allies to make terminating a pregnancy a rare and mournful event. The woman who makes that decision will be helped through her loss and will not be abused or stigmatized. But if our plan works, there will be very few abortions.

THE WHOLE DRIFT OF THIS OBU THING
IS TO SHATTER THE OLIGARCHY!

OBU asks the "pro-life" assemblies, are you with us in this mission to minimize abortion? And you know–be honest–that even when it's a crime, abortions will be done. With the policies of life that we enact together, there will be fewer *legal* abortions than there would otherwise be *illegal* ones. So, what do you say? Let's do it, for–OBU was about to say, "for Christ's sake" in its vernacular sense; but let us say it here in its theological sense: for Christ's sake; or, conversely, Let's fuckin' do it, ok? L'chaim, already.

BUT THAT CAN ONLY BE DONE
THROUGH SOME REAL, EXPANDED FORM
OF SOLIDARITY: OBU

OBU Manifesto #41

What, OBU wonders, should universities do in the current moment? What should university faculties do?

University faculty must help the university understand itself. The elite private university must be helped to understand its place in the oligarchy, and must be helped in disentangling itself. Public and non-elite universities must see themselves as public goods whose public nature must be protected and nurtured.

The university must demonstrate an *unambiguous* support for justice. It must be in the front of this struggle, not dragged equivocating and calculating its public relations campaign. The university must be a bastion of intellectual and moral integrity in a political moment when both are in short supply.

If it is not that, OBU wonders, then what is it? What is the university meant for?

Intellectual clarity is a pillar of social justice, just as truth is one leg of the three-legged universe.

The university must reject hypocrisy and expediency.

OBU modestly suggests that university officials who hold their fingers to the wind should lose their fingers.

No, no; that's a metaphor. OBU is not anti-digital.

The situation, of course, is complicated, OBU acknowledges. The wealthy private universities are deeply entangled in the oligarchy. They are products and pillars of oligarchy. Their fortunes often derived from and were augmented by slavery. They produce leaders of capital. Their alumni and donors are masters of the economic and political structures.

But now, the Trumpist moment requires a reorientation. Who really are the university's friends? Is it necessarily the large donors? The university gets to build a new Center for Whatever (whether it truly needs it or not), but what are the larger goals of that fortune that makes the university so fortunate? Who, OBU asks again, are the university's friends?

The university, OBU maintains, must support labor. It must stop opposing unions for its workers. It must stop hiring expensive, union-busting law firms that harass and insult its workers. It must support the rights and livelihoods of workers throughout its whole community. In the current political moment in which the rights of workers are under direct attack and siege, the university must position itself without equivocation on the side of workers.

In the current moment, OBU says, if the university is not on the side of labor, it is on the side of Trump. The university must be made to understand this. It is not enough to make mostly empty statements about protecting its immigrant students. Of course it must do this, insofar as it's able. But it must side with its workers. This is the harder task, and the more crucial in the long run. Most immigrants, after all, are here not to study but to work.

Just as the universities before the Civil War were *all* implicated in the profits of slavery and its products, so today they are all implicated in the profits of plutocracy. A generation or so from now, this association will seem as shameful as the association with slavery seems to us today. How, our descendants will ask, could our university have accepted money from so-and-so? How could it have invested in this or that company? Did the university really have no moral compass whatever?

And what should the faculty do? First, the faculty should insist that the university fulfill its ethical obligations towards its workers, towards it town or city, and towards the nation and the world. The faculty will help the university reimagine its financial orientations. If the university behaves better, it if begins to detach itself from the oligarchy and its interests, how will it sustain itself?

Second, OBU suggests, university faculty should be encouraged to act as full citizens in the polity. Their scholarly expertise is sometimes of crucial value; but sometimes–often, in the Age of Trump–academic workers should act simply as citizens and human beings. Be in the movement to fight oligarchy. Be part of the growing solidarity.

OBU recommends that faculty members'civic engagement should be a criterion for tenure along with scholarship and teaching.

Ambivalent (Anti-)OBU Interlude

Is it not possible for OBU to stop talking?

What's the point? Who is talking and who is listening?

Can OBU not just shut up?

It's getting in the way.

It pontificates.

It's a big lubricant, but nothing is sliding.

What does OBU know?

Nothing.

What does OBU think?

Who cares.

What is this *union* it claims to be synthesizing?

The "Movement that Does not Exist"!

Well, that's for sure!

And OBU thinks that OBU is the way to get there?!

By quoting William Blake and Walt Whitman?!?

By saying, "we need some new kind of solidarity yet unimagined and untried"!

And we need to reconceive the labor movement

And to teach liberals how not to be ineffectual twits

And to teach conservatives how not to be mean-spirited assholes.

OBU will shove poetry out of the ingrown institutions and into the greater polis

And convince the auto industry to go all-electric and the energy industry to go all-renewable and convince the meat industry basically to disappear... i.e. to go entirely organic/free range

And move economists to imagine an economy of equitably distributed prosperity without relying on ecologically destructive "growth."

So, why can't OBU stop talking?

Why can't OBU actually get something done?

Stop complaining. Are there rooms available? Put people in them.

Imagine and create solidarities. Of course it's difficult.

Begin.

OBU Manifesto #42

OBU IS TRUDGING. IT IS TIME FOR THE TRUDGE. WITHIN EACH TRUDGE IS THE BRILLIANT flash. Or perhaps within every third or fifth trudge is the insane, precipitate, knowledge and the revelatory warmth, the feeling of connectedness with other souls. And around each flash of truth must congeal the trudge. It's the trudge that hauls for the body and the wheels, the architecture, the ability to withstand exhaustion and failure. The brilliant flash is both momentary and eternal. The trudge endures through time.

The trudge of the endless meetings; the moment finally when we have a plan and we're going to do it and keep doing it; the coordinated phone calls; the dinner with the group in another neighborhood or city; the emergency call that someone is being detained by immigration officers; the meeting with the congressperson or the state rep; the alliance of the union with the environmental group; the address to the disappointed wavering Trumpistas, and maybe two of them join you; the joining together of workers, either with or without a union, the commitment that the company will make no significant decision without the workers being part of that process; the united force of cities upon giant corporate "non-profit" entities like hospitals and universities that they contribute justly toward the cities that host them and provide them with land, labor, utilities, safe neighborhoods, clean air and water, transportation; the collective trudge that brings power to people to determine the conditions of their lives.

The acrobatic leap and twist is part of the trudge. The joy of returning home having accomplished something is part of the trudge. Just the general task of life, of job and family and various enjoyments and fulfilling responsibilities, and being exhausted most of the time and being just plain sick of the whole thing and will you stop calling me, I'm tired of it, and taking the dog for a walk, getting the oil changed, suddenly having to shell out 400 or 800 bucks for repairing something or other and there's always something, and the trudge is the something that there always is. And how the hell are you supposed to do it, I mean on a continual basis, which is the standard basis; you don't generally have a choice of reducing it to something less than continual.

And the trudge is both the vision and the journey toward the vision. The journey and the vision and the work are always intertwined. And the trudge is the twine.

"The profound change has come upon them. Rooted, they grip down and begin to awaken."

OBU is and will not stop.

OBU is not about everyone thinking the same thing. Sharing a few important commitments will be enough. It's ok if you don't like *La La Land*; and it's ok if you do like *La La Land*. If you don't like *Fences*, there might be a problem.

The trajectories indicated here do not stop at the end of this sentence or of this page. The energies here, both in the writing and in the reading, are propelled beyond themselves. They fly out, do reconnaissance in the future and return with vital intel.

And we'll ask ourselves when the OBU Inter-temporal Knowledge Drone returns, is that where we want to go?

ONE BIG UNION UNITED TO BUST OLIGARCHY AND CREATE DEMOCRACY

What we need to know, OBU suggests, is known... all but one thing.